Architecture in Perspective

11ᵗʰ Annual International Competition of Architectural Perspectivists

The American Society of Architectural Perspectivists

Published by Rockport Publishers
146 Granite Street
Rockport, Massachusetts 01966-1299
ISBN 1-56496-300-4

Cover Photo: Paul Stevenson Oles FAIA, p.9
Back Cover Photos (top to bottom): Hisae Shoda, p.11
Willem van den Hoed, p.13

Contents

Editor
Gordon Grice OAA, MRAIC, Toronto

Additional Copy
Thomas Wells Schaller AIA, New York

Notes Supplied By
Frank M. Costantino, Winthrop, MA
William J. Mitchell, Cambridge, MA
Steve Oles FAIA, Newton, MA
Tamotsu Yamamoto and John Sheehy FAIA, Boston

ASAP wishes to thank the following individuals whose
dedication to their tasks went far beyond the call of duty:
Arthur Furst, editor at Rockport Publishing
John Deputy, MetroDesign

**We would especially like to thank Otis Elevator
Company for their continuing encouragement
and financial support.**

Foreword

It is my great privilege to serve the membership of American Society of Architectural Perspectivists as President during the year in which we enter our second decade as an organization, and to acknowledge the dedication and energies of those who have served as Board members since its founding, and all members who have participated in ASAP's activities and programs.

For twelve years, I have kept a copy of the announcement of the "First Annual Architectural Delineators Show" held here in this city at the Boston Architectural Center in September of 1984. It was our first group exhibition of the work of professional architectural illustrators, and it was the beginning of ASAP. The 16'×18' space was crammed with renderings—mostly small color photographs of the work of local illustrators, many of whom met for the first time that day. After spending hours putting up the work, we viewed the exhibition, shook hands, and took it all down again. How could any of us have guessed that from this modest four-hour exhibition would eventually develop a four week exhibition that travels worldwide for forty weeks and features the work of four hundred members from twenty-four countries on four continents!

Changes followed swiftly: In 1986 we gained national status and a logo for our letterhead, a home at the BAC, and 470 submissions from 125 members representing 28 states. Our scope soon turned international, and we enjoyed the participation of representatives from the Japan Architectural Renderers Association. Soon members from Australia, Austria, Brunei, China, Denmark, England, France, Germany, Greece, Holland, Hong Kong, Indonesia, Israel, Japan, Korea, New Zealand, the Philippines, Portugal, Singapore, Sweden, Taiwan, and Thailand as well as neighbors from Canada and Mexico joined our ranks.

ASAP members have also been invited to participate in events held in England, with the Society of Architectural and Industrial Illustrators; in Japan, every year, with the Japan Architectural Renderers Association; the Architectural Society of China in 1992; and the Korean Architectural Perspective Association in 1995.

Over the years, we have viewed, admired, and studied each other's work and techniques, and during this time, a great fellowship has developed among us based on the common language we share. This is the language of rendering. Since 1986, when the work was largely straightforward, a new body of "imaginary" work has evolved, brought about not merely by skills, but by ideas.

Still, I find that I increasingly struggle to define rendering and its place in visual expression. No matter what character it takes on, rendering at its heart is the kind of drawing made specifically to give visual form to an architect's or designer's ideas and concepts. Renderers must painstakingly develop keen skills in depicting surfaces, reflections, and architectural materials, and be able to blend color and apply line with deftness and precision. Above all, renderers must be flawless in the mastery of "perspective mechanics."

Perspective has been a visualization tool since its discovery in Italy at the start of the Renaissance, but it is only that: a tool in the artist's repertoire—a way to give scale and place to subjects having nothing, ultimately, to do with such mechanics. For renderers, perspective is the subject. The artists of the Renaissance, and those that followed, have at times embraced or rejected perspective as an embodiment of "realism" which may, or may not, echo the issues and interests of their times. Renderers can never decide to abandon perspective. It is their image. Artists themselves have historically acted as the visual "voice" of their times. As such, they express their beliefs through art, and participate in redefining contemporary society. It is not surprising, therefore, that artists, writers, and poets have been at times deified or destroyed because of their power to influence society, having as they do the unique means to move and inform those who view their work. And their work lives on, long after the politicians are dead. So, to me, the definition of an artist is someone who is the visual / intellectual spokesman or commentator of one's time. One's ideas, and not one's skills, are at the heart of one's creativity and one's legacy.

When we judge rendering, what are we judging? Is it creativity? Originality? If so, where does the creativity lie? Is it art or illustration? Are we judging the architectural design? Of course not. Are we judging a renderer's concepts, or one's philosophy of architecture? Of course not. Perhaps we are judging levels of skill, coloring techniques, or composition. I struggle throughout the process, year after year, trying to discover what is rendering, and who are renderers.

Our conventions and seminars over these past ten years have been focused on technical issues and members' discoveries about the manipulation of the various media at our disposal. Our inquiries about each other's work, and about rendering in general, concern the question "How?" not "Why?" or "What?". Because we are perhaps "Renderers" after all, hired to represent another's concepts (although, in many cases, the "concepts" are our own).

In our work as professional renderers, we strive to bring creativity and beauty to our assignment as our way of creating something more than a mere visual model, and through our skills lend impact that will enhance the work of the architect. So, while we may be, in the words of Mr. Henry Cobb FAIA, "the servants of servants," we have every right to enjoy professional pride and personal satisfaction, to believe that we have brought artistry (if not art) to each project, and know that whatever renderings are—or aren't—we have given every ounce of our talent and intelligence to our chosen life's work.

Tamotsu Yamamoto
President, American Society of Architectural Perspectivists
Boston, March 1996

First Annual Architectural Delineators Show

Boston Architectural Center
320 Newbury Street
Boston, Massachusetts
Thursday, 20 September 1984, 4:00–8:00 PM

Venues

Feature image from the AIP Call-for-entries Poster: Symphony Hall Boston
Architects: McKim Mead & White; Illustrator: ascribed to Theodore O. Langerfeldt (d. 1906)

The Boston Architectural Center
Boston, Massachusetts
October 24–November 9, 1996

Mount Ida College
Boston, Massachusetts
November 22–December 19, 1996

AIA Nevada Chapter Gallery
Reno, Nevada
December 1996–January 1997

AIA National Convention
New Orleans, Louisiana
May 16–19, 1997

Introduction

The work contained in this book is the product of a small group of professionals: members of the American Society of Architectural Perspectivists. The great majority of these individuals are commercial renderers, and they are located almost everywhere on the globe. Some of their work may have been commissioned by well-known architects to depict landmark buildings, others by lesser-known professionals whose modest proposals might require an experienced illustrator to highlight subtle attributes. In some cases, the drawings serve as explorations of ideas suggested by the illustrators themselves, in others by designers who need a skilled hand to present their work while it is still on the boards, or drifting formlessly in their heads.

Frequently, the work is so masterfully executed that it enters the realm of fine art and deserves to be evaluated according to its aesthetic merits alone. The annual *Architecture in Perspective* exhibition presents such an opportunity. Illustrators submit their drawings in the form of slides to be viewed and appraised by a three-person jury which, like the city in which the judging occurs, changes every year. The jurors are selected from allied professions, such as architecture, planning, academia, photography, fine art, and illustration. The product of the intensive one-day adjudication takes the form of a travelling exhibition which circulates between 50 and 60 renderings around the world, a catalogue, a copy of which you now hold, and a new standard of excellence for the architectural illustrators of the world.

Because ASAP is constituted as an affinity group and not a professional organization, it is an *inclusive* not *exclusive* association. Anyone who wishes to become a member of our society can and should do so. The society has managed, in its brief life so far, to elevate our occupation to the status of a profession without ever resorting to an "ivory tower" mentality. With ASAP's direct encouragement and participation, an international network of renderers has taken form, with a spirit of co-operation and mutual support that is unique.

The idea of a renderers' affiliation was first conceived in 1975. In that year, two Boston-area renderers, Frank M. Costantino and Steve Oles FAIA commenced a four-year teaching engagement at the Rhode Island School of Design. As Frank puts it, "Discussions about work and drawing were part of our growing friendship." A variety of other factors kept the discussions alive until, in 1983, Steve and Frank again wound up side by side, this time at Harvard's Graduate School of Design. With the additional participation of colleague Stephen W. Rich AIA, sufficient courage was summoned to consider mounting a show. "The worthiness of the idea was clearly evident, but the circumstances for developing it did not occur until July 1984, when the three of us agreed that an attempt would be worth the effort." The show lasted only four hours, but the response was favorable enough that a month-long exhibit was mounted the following year. By this time, the show's reach extended from Maine to Pennsylvania with the addition of eight original drawings from Australia, giving the first hint of international interest. "In 1986, we became national, with an ASAP logo, letterhead, and address at the BAC," says President and charter member Tamotsu Yamamoto. The American Society of Architectural Perspectivists was officially born.

In the ten years since our official birth, our activities have moved far beyond the Boston city limits. Our membership has expanded, despite the first "A" in our initials, to include a large percentage of non-Americans, and our conventions have moved about the continent from coast to coast. The yearly *Architecture in Perspective* exhibition has begun to travel more and more widely, including Europe last year, and Asia this year. Our books and catalogues are distributed and sold throughout the world. But there's no question that our heart remains in Boston.

So, as our second decade begins, we are back in Boston. To add icing to the cake, Bostonian charter member Mongkol Tansantisuk AIA has captured a Juror's Award, and the Ferriss Prize, our most prestigious honour, has been awarded this year to none other than Bostonian co-founder Steve Oles.

AIP 1 jurors, left to right, William Kirby Lockard FAIA;
A. Anthony Tappe FAIA; and Brian Burr

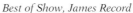

Best of Show, James Record   *Best of Show, Lee Dunnette AIA*

Jury Report

As in previous years, the entries for the ASAP *Architecture in Perspective* awards were numerous and of very high quality. The jurors (John Sheehy FAIA, Toshihiro Katayama, and William J. Mitchell) viewed the 478 images that were submitted, in slide form, on a cold, gray day in Boston. Discussions of the work began over coffee and bagels in the morning, continued over lunchtime bento boxes, and did not wrap up until well into the evening—when exhausted jurors and ASAP officials and staff eventually forsook this perspective cornucopia for the Cornucopia restaurant.

The jurors were particularly struck by the geographic diversity of the entries and by the vivid snapshot that (taken as a whole) they provided into the current state of architecture worldwide. The majority of the entries were from North America (including strong representation from Canada), but there were numerous excellent entries from Europe and Australia as well as many parts of Asia—ranging from Japan to the Philippines. The current intensity of architectural activity in China and in East Asia generally was reflected in the large number of images of projects in that region. In addition to the expected public, commercial, and residential buildings, there were lots of large, mixed-use projects, surprisingly many transportation subjects (airports, railway stations, roadways, bridges), and quite a few churches—mostly, for some reason, empty.

Then, there were the seagulls. Lots and lots of seagulls! Too many seagulls! For a while, we formed the working hypothesis that the success of an image might be inversely proportional to the number of seagulls appearing in it, but this didn't consistently check out. In any case, we offer this advice to next year's entrants: "Hold the seagulls!"

Instructions, of course, were to focus on the quality of the perspective representations and disregard the quality of the architecture represented. The jurors did their best to stick to this principle, and I think succeeded pretty well, but that wasn't always easy! On some gratifying occasions—for example, in Steve Oles's brilliant delineation of a breathtaking office tower by Harry Cobb (the Hugh Ferriss Memorial Prize Winner)—the quality of the architecture was consistent with the quality of its representation. No problem there. But there were some other moments (and I won't name names!) when the jurors sat in frozen horror as a superb image of some architectural monster flashed onto the screen—leaving us admiring the skill of the perspectivist but hoping that the project would never see the light of day. This raises, of course, one of the ethical dilemmas that perspectivists must sometimes face: if you know that the building that you're asked to draw is a dog, should you use your skills

to flatter it as much as possible, should you be more objective and perhaps risk the wrath of your client or employer, or should you just politely decline the job? Answers to such questions are not always straightforward, but being prepared to reflect on them where necessary, and being ready to take a firm stand where it's called for, are among the crucial differences between the ethical professionalism that ASAP encourages and mere hack-work.

It was encouraging to see that diverse graphic traditions continue to thrive, and have their talented adherents. We saw many masters of the pencil, with finely tuned skills in registering the variations, graduations, and contrasts of value across a scene. We saw that the ancient art of watercolor shows no signs of fading away, and we were frequently delighted by the delicacy of a wash or the luminosity and sparkle that only transparency can bring. And we saw opaque media deployed with impeccable precision and control.

The role of the computer was even more evident than it has been in recent years. No doubt this is due, in large part, to ongoing decreases in the cost of computation, to continued advances in CAD (Computer Assisted Design) and rendering software, and to growing use among architects and illustrators of three-dimensional geometric modeling software that makes a computer model (rather than information on paper) available as the perspective's starting point. But it is also due to the fact that sophisticated CAD and rendering technology, today, is sufficiently straightforward to use that it does not have to be in the hands of technical specialists, and can be employed directly by artists who have the knowledge, insight, and sensibility to make it really sing. If you look carefully at the computer-based work among this year's crop of entries you can clearly see the emergence of some committed craftsmanship and an embryonic artistic tradition.

Be careful, though! In the past, computer-generated perspectives could often be identified immediately by their harsh and mechanical look, by their crude coloring, and by their cartoonish detail. You could dismiss many of them as low-grade Nintendo imagery. That is no longer necessarily the case, since the technology has improved dramatically, since the available computer tools have become better understood and more discerningly used, and since a variety of hybrid computer/manual techniques have emerged. Sometimes it is very difficult to detect whether a computer has been involved in the production of an image at all.

Consider some of the computer/manual hybrid possibilities—most of which are represented among this year's entries. First, you can use the computer (now, often, in real time) to explore possible perspective station points and other

William J. Mitchell

Toshihiro Katayama

John P. Sheehy, FAIA

parameters, then employ a computer-generated plot as an underlay for production of a final image in pencil, airbrush, or whatever traditional medium you might choose. Second, you can employ an accurate, physically-based lighting simulation technique such as radiosity rendering to calculate the tonal values on surfaces, then replicate these values in a hand-generated image. Third, you can use digital "paint" software (such as Photoshop) to manipulate computer-generated images, to add detail by hand, to insert scale figures and landscape elements, and so on. And, finally, you can use combinations of texture mapping, digital filtering, and printing technology to generate images that have the wonderful variety of strokes, grains, and microstructures that have traditionally been produced by pencils and other manual tools encountering textured drawing surfaces.

When the jurors reflected on the range of work that they had seen, they were impressed by the variety of intentions and purposes that it represented. There were quick design sketches that recorded the process of speculatively probing an idea. There were precise, careful studies of mass and surface in urban or landscape context. There were sober, careful images that were intended to function as the most accurate possible predictions of the appearances of fully developed designs. There were seductive sales jobs for brochures and boardroom presentations. And, of course, there were fantasies, jokes, and whimsical fictions.

The award-winning entries reflected this diversity of intention, provenance, and technique. Willem van den Hoed's winning entry in the sketch category is literally a page from a diary—a freeze-frame of one precise moment in an architect's ongoing exploration of spatial and massing possibilities. Toshihiro Katayama chose, for his juror's award, Anna Melissa Harris's gestural, painterly interpretation of some simple, dramatic, architectural volumes. By contrast, John Sheehy's juror's award went to Mongkol Tansantisuk's wonderfully delicate and precise rendition of materiality and detailing in the three street facades of the Suffolk County Courthouse. For my juror's award, I picked out Serge Zaleski's vivid and energetic bird's-eye, cutaway view of a cinema lobby. Hisae Shoda's winning entry in the formal category is specially memorable for the way that it evokes the magic of moving, lighted forms—particularly a huge, roof-top Ferris wheel. And the Ferriss prize went not to the Ferris wheel (what a spin that would have given!) but to a Steve Oles monochrome, pencil masterpiece that, coincidentally, evokes memories of Ferriss himself—a sheer, shining tower that rises out of shadowy masses to gleam against the dark sky.

William J. Mitchell
Dean, School of Architecture & Planning, M.I.T.

The Architects Building, 52 Broad Street, Boston

Peter Vanderwarker

The Architects Building Members' Lounge, 5th floor

Steve Rosenthal

The Hugh Ferriss Memorial Prize

Superlatives are nothing rare in describing the work of Paul Stevenson Oles FAIA. He has, quite literally, set the standard of quality for at least an entire generation of architectural artists; and in a great many ways, it has been on his shoulders that many of us have stood to attain our own place in the profession. So, it is a fitting tribute and a richly deserved honor that has been accorded Oles by the *Architecture in Perspective 11* jury in naming him as the recipient of the Hugh Ferriss Memorial Prize.

As a founder of the American Society of Architectural Perspectivists, the organization which originated and fosters the coveted Ferriss Prize, Oles has finally been inducted as a member of a rather exclusive club which, ironically, would not exist without his efforts. Few know more profoundly than Oles himself the elusiveness of this honor. Although it could be argued for any number of reasons that he has rightly deserved this honor (an unparalleled body of consistently exceptional work and his ceaseless efforts on behalf of the profession, to name two), it can more accurately be said that, through the sometimes brutal AIP jury process, he has truly earned it. Moreover, where he might be seen to be deserving of praise for his incomparable legacy of leadership, scholarship, and draftsmanship, he has earned this specific accolade upon the merits of a single outstanding drawing: his interpretation of a Paris office tower designed by Henry N. Cobb FAIA. Of course, within the realm of this work can be seen the elements of that legacy come to fruition.

From the very first stages of the AIP 11 selection process, this particular piece was recognized by all three jurors as a serious contender for the top prize. "This piece," juror Sheehy said simply, "is Ferriss material." Indeed it was. Juror Mitchell remarked on its compelling nature and juror Sheehy further praised its "brilliant technique." All three jurors succinctly labelled it a "classic" when considering the unassailable confidence evidenced by its composition and execution. It is, in fact, the concept of the "classic drawing" that may most have shaped Ole's own conception of this piece from the outset, at least in the sense that the phrase is manifest in the work of Hugh Ferriss himself. While Oles lays no claim to being "this generation's Ferriss," he does not hesitate to admit to being "powerfully influenced, fascinated, and inspired by Ferriss's work." Writes Oles: "I have a large poster of his famous 1922 Setback Zoning Study #4 (the image gracing—in stylized form—the Ferriss medallion) which, in the opinion of his daughter, Jean Ferriss Leich, is the most characteristic work of his career. This is not only an homage, but a shameless attempt to allow my work to be osmotically ameliorated by the presence of this masterpiece."

It is Steve Oles himself who has noted a "remarkable resemblance in general composition, format, and graphic character" between his rendition of Cobb's tower and an especially powerful Ferriss work, the Center of Philosophy from 1928. "The list of similarities between the two buildings and especially their images," writes Oles, "is impressive: The Philosophy tower design is based on a geometric floor plate comprised of the intersecting polygons; the Paris tower on intersecting arcs. The dark sky context (night in the Ferriss, ambiguous in the Paris image) foils a single shimmering, asymmetrically-placed shaft in a decidedly vertical format." Many other similarities are also noted by Oles, including eye level, point of view, treatment of context, and proportion.

But perhaps the most striking similarity between the two works (as well as between the body of work of these two artists) is the strength of the conception, the authority of the image of a commanding building form upon the landscape, and the facility to consistently communicate a complete impression of that structural form to the viewer. In both these specific images, we can, of course, see something of what the buildings are in a physical sense, but more importantly, we are able to glimpse something of what they may be: their emotional impact, their spirit, the "full truth" about which Ferriss so often spoke.

Concerning our profession, Oles writes: "We are products of our temporal and professional context, just as Hugh Ferriss was of his. I'm sure I speak for all perspectivists today when I say that we're particularly grateful for the precedents, the insights, and the profound inspiration of the 'patron saint' of our maturing profession, the legendary Hugh Ferriss." We congratulate Steve Oles on this current honor and remind him that much of what he writes about Hugh Ferriss can be, and often is, said of him as well.

"Philosophy," Hugh Ferriss, 1928
Image courtesy of the Avery Library, Columbia University

Paul Stevenson Oles FAIA

Interface Architects
One Gateway Center, Suite 501 A
Newton, MA 02158
617-527-6790

Hines France Office Tower
Henry N. Cobb FAIA; Pei Cobb Freed & Partners

Black waxbase pencil on vellum, 13 x 8, 1995

Formal Category Award

"Atmosphere" may well be the word that most readily comes to mind when viewing this exceptional airbrush work of Hisae Shoda. In fact, a convincing sense of atmosphere may be the single most valid concept in an attempt to explain the success of much of the growing body of work completed by her which is becoming increasingly familiar to the audience of *Architecture in Perspective* exhibitions.

While the overall sense of atmosphere, largely created by the skillful manipulation of the graphic representation of the effects of light impressed the AIP 11 jurors, they were not immune to the other compelling qualities in Shoda's piece. Citing the work's power, simplicity of elements, and compellingly hot color scheme, they were also moved by the "dynamic quality of the composition" and, moreover, the "strong sense of movement" implied by the juxtaposition of warm and cool tonalities, the horizontal and vertical elements and, to say the very least, the kinetics implied by the graphic treatment of the moving Ferris wheel, train, and automobiles.

It is a testament to the artist's considerable skill that the apparent economy and simplicity of elements utilized here belie a sophisticated conception and technical control that seem to serve perfectly the needs of the drawing's narrative. It should not be forgotten that this piece represents an amusement facility (a first, incidently, for an AIP competition prize winner). The choices made by the artist with respect to composition, color, kinetics, and dynamic range seem perfectly appropriate to the subject matter. It is likely that the same choices would not work—nor would an artist of Shoda's skill have expected them to—for a scheme of another character, such as a governmental building or a residential complex. There are, unquestionably, profound lessons in the art of "choice" and "appropriateness" to be gained from a close study of this exceptional piece.

With the designation of Shoda's Formal Category Award in AIP 11, it becomes increasingly evident that the internationalism of ASAP as a society and AIP as a viable forum for architectural artwork worldwide is firmly established. Certainly, the talent of many of our Japanese colleagues in AIP exhibitions over the past several years has been a force commanding respect and attention. However, the suggestion of the emergence of somewhat nationalistic artistic voices should not dismiss the clearly articulated individualism of one voice. Recognition of this piece by the gifted artist Hisae Shoda is testament to that.

Hisae Shoda
Takenaka Corporation
8-24-305, 2 Chome Deguchi
Hirakata-shi, Osaka 573
Japan
81-720-35-2690

Hankyu Five Project
Takenaka Corporation

Airbrush, acrylic, 28 x 20, 1996

Sketch Category Award

Ever since the Informal or "Sketch" category was added to the *Architecture in Perspective* competition several years ago, the discussion has raged. What constitutes a sketch? How does it differ from a "finished" work? How do we deal with drawings that refuse to fall into any category? This year's AIP jury faced the same dilemma in attempting to sort through and sort out the copious entries in the Sketch Category. Fortunately, the remarkable work by Dutch architect/artist Willem van den Hoed left no doubt in the jury's mind regarding its claim to the Sketch Category nor its exceptional graphic merits.

After examining all points of view in the Formal vs. Informal debate, a consensus can usually be reached that, if nothing else, a sketch is principally concerned with the drawing process. In the drawing of van den Hoed, the element of process virtually jumps from the page. The jury loved the "rough and ready" quality of the diminutive work, while praising the many spontaneous subjective decisions, such as the striking use of color and the dominant perspective angularity, which seems to take its departure from the torn lower left corner of the page.

Regardless of their appeal, these graphic devices would mean little without the wealth of design information contained in the dashed lines and hasty marker colors applied with astonishing economy and clarity. The drawing gives the impression of an architectural thought developing before our eyes like a Polaroid photograph. Equally fascinating to the jury was the fact that the piece was executed on the page of a small pocket diary with type and extraneous notations in van den Hoed's native Dutch. There is a subtle but insistent sense of both time and place super- (or sub-) imposed on the work, giving an immediacy and complete lack of the pretence or "preciousness" that sometimes characterizes more formal, premeditated, and circumspect works.

Willem van den Hoed is a relatively new face on the international architectural illustration scene (an equally minuscule and equally exceptional drawing appeared in AIP 9). It seems certain, however, that one possessed of such an intuitive design and graphic sense will provide us with many more ingenious and appetizing drawings in exhibitions to come.

1995 maart

Week 11 – Maand 3

Wk	9	10	11	12	13	14
Ma	27	6	13	20	27	3
Di	28	7	14	21	28	4
Wo	1	8	15	22	29	5
Do	2	9	16	23	30	6
Vr	3	10	17	24	31	7
Za	4	11	18	25	1	8
Zo	5	12	19	26	2	9

13 maandag

erger dan over de tong gaan:
doodgezwegen worden.

Willem van den Hoed
1000 Huizen
Lange Geer 44, Delft 2611 PW
The Netherlands
31-1521-33382

Housing Study
Self-commissioned

Markers and pencil, 6 x 4, 1995

Juror's Award

As is often the case, the three Juror's Award winning drawings are strikingly dissimilar. This is both an accurate indicator of the amazing range of imagery from which the jury had to select, and an interesting reflection of the interests and predilections of the individual jury members.

Jury chairman William J. Mitchell, Dean of the School of Architecture and Planning at M.I.T., was greatly impressed by some of the computer-generated imagery that appeared among the entries. His comments, based on his experience in digital communications, were much appreciated by the other jury members. For his Juror's Award, however, he selected a masterful work executed without any benefit of computer wizardry and in a traditional opaque medium that may have appealed to a possibly more deep-rooted passion: homeland.

Coincidentally, the recipient of juror Mitchell's Award selection is, like himself, a native of Melbourne, Australia. Architect/illustrator Serge Zaleski FSAI, ARAIA another relative new-comer to the AIP fold, has exhibited once before, in AIP 10. His submissions to AIP 11 seem to possess a sort of subliminal Australian quality that Serge himself has attributed to a certain "theatricality," and "the result of living in a land of harsh colors." In one of his entries (the selection appearing in the back of this book), the Australian nature is palpable: it shows an aboriginal music group (Gondwanaland) performing near a "humpy" in a fictional location in the Australian outback.

For the award-winning piece, however, ethno-cultural qualities aside, the appeal can be attributed more directly to the masterful use of technique to convey both clarity and excitement in an elaborately informative drawing. The work is mostly a construct from Zaleski's imagination. In commissioning the prototype theater complex with themed lobby, the client, Hoyts International, provided a "script" rather than design drawings. The complex forms, inter-relationships, and visual effects that lend the drawing its appeal were devised within the course of the illustration process.

For his Juror's Award, international architect John Sheehy FAIA chose a drawing from a much less distant locale. In fact, a short walk from the Boston Society of Architects, a large copy of the same drawing currently graces the construction hoarding of a building site. The masterful drawing by ASAP veteran Mongkol Tansantisuk AIA depicts a proposal for the new Suffolk County Court House, by architects Kallmann, McKinnell and Wood, located next to the Boston City Hall, a few blocks from the jury room. Sheehy's own words speak eloquently about the appeal of Tansantisuk's fine black-and-white pencil drawing:

"This drawing is in the tradition of the renderings of Jay Henderson Barr and [1996 Ferriss Winner] Steve Oles. The drawing has minimum line work and is made up mostly of of tonal values. The rendering of light and dark values creates the illusion of three-dimensionality that represents light and shadow and gives an illusion of color.

"This drawing carefully places the new courthouse in context with [the Massachusetts State Service Center designed by Paul Rudolph], wrapping around it on either side. The establishment of vanishing points is complex because the site, like most sites in the city of Boston, is irregular and therefore this building fills an irregular acute-angled corner. Often, this condition leads to exaggerated vanishing points that contribute to the lack of understanding of the true condition. Here, we see three elevations of an object that are skillfully toned to fold around three corners. The site too is not flat and the drawing skillfully deals with the perspective of a slight hill."

The success of the image is all the more impressive when one considers that Tansantisuk's decision to render the image only in black-and-white was due to severe time constraints: it was created in only two or three days.

Toshihiro Katayama was the jury's non-architect. As director for the Center for the Visual Arts at Harvard University, and as a professor, painter, and environmental artist, his background has exposed him to a great deal of architectural and non-architectural artwork. Clearly, the sensibilities that he exercised during the AIP jury selection were those of a fine artist. In making his selection for Juror's Award, he was swayed by the strong emotive power of some of the images, and less concerned with technical virtuosity.

The piece which he has selected, a haunting image by Anna Melissa Harris RA, has an unquestionable emotional appeal. Interestingly, Harris, an assistant professor of architecture in Ann Arbor, Michigan, uses words in describing her work that are similar to Katayama's. She strives in her drawing and painting to create a "sensational experience," i.e., one that appeals more directly to the sentience of the viewer than to the intellect. In her words, drawing is most frequently a means of establishing an "analytical base to help refine my methods of formal analysis." Even her media, oil pastel and oil paint, are seldom those of the renderer. The impetus for this piece, entitled *Transylvania Farm Buildings*, did in fact come from impressions gathered during a train trip through Rumanian Transylvania. The execution of the drawing was subsequently occasioned by a request from her sister in Virginia for help in siting a new home in relation to existing farm buildings. In this particular work, Harris wished to establish a "radiance" that emanated from the subject by using bright colors as a base, and overlaying a dinginess reminiscent of the view through the windows of a train. In addition, the jostling of form and color gives the piece a dynamism that is not often found in formal architectural drawings.

The distinction that frequently appears to exist between rendering and fine art was foremost in juror Katayama's mind. He states: "I hope to see more renderers break the barrier between fine art and rendering." Many of us in the rendering community share his sentiments, and are attempting in our own ways to accomplish this feat. We salute Harris's obvious success in this endeavor and hope to see much more of her work in future AIP exhibits.

Serge Zaleski FSAI, ARAIA
Delineation Graphix
238 Bulwara Road
Ultimo, Sydney NSW 2007
Australia
612-552-3666

Prototype Multiple Cinema Lobby
Belt Collins Australia / Attractions International

Tempera and watercolor, 1995

Mongkol Tansantisuk AIA
Architectural Presentations
672 Grove Street
Newton, MA 02162-1319
617-332-7885

New Suffolk County Trial Court Facility
Kallmann, McKinnell & Wood Architects

Waxbase pencil, 16 x 16, 1994

A. Melissa Harris RA
University of Michigan
College of Architecture & Urban Planning
2000 Bonisteel Blvd.
Ann Arbor, MI 48109
313-936-0224

Transylvania Farm Buildings
Wren + Barry Batterton

Oil pastel, 15 x 21, 1993

Awards of Excellence

The drawings in the following pages constitute the remaining 47 of the 53 drawings and paintings chosen by our judges as the best entries from the 478 submitted to *Architecture in Perspective 11*. Along with the six prize winners, these works will form this year's traveling exhibition.

We have, over the past decade, discussed numerous methods of categorizing our submissions. Suggestions made by our members and jurors have been debated at length, but every system has its flaws: the more complicated the system, the deeper the faults. To keep things simple, submissions to the *Architecture in Perspective* jury are divided into two categories only: Formal and Sketch.

This distinction is made for two reasons: firstly, to encourage illustrators to submit drawings regardless of their degree of polish and realism, and secondly, to free the judges from the necessity to judge all drawings by the same criteria. While entrants are required to designate in which category their work belongs, jurors are free to recategorize drawings as they may see fit.

Formal Category

Formal drawings are generally considered to be those which are dimensionally accurate, graphically descriptive, and tending toward a "realistic" representation. At times, drawings which demonstrate none of these characteristics, but are done in a careful or deliberate way are also deemed to be formal drawings. The 39 Awards of Excellence which comprise this section include highly realistic perspective renderings, as well as orthographic drawings and collages; drawings which are client-commissioned along with self-commissioned works; images executed on a computer, and renderings done by hand in a wide variety of media.

Sketch Category

Following the Formal Category Winners are the eight Informal or Sketch Category Winners. Informal drawings, or Sketches, are considered to be anything that doesn't fall neatly into the Formal category. Typically, these drawings are the result of a technique rapidly applied that captures the essence of an idea, often before it has been clearly articulated in the mind of the creator. Understandably, sketches are frequently the product of the building designer, who may or may not be a professional illustrator. But there are any number of other kinds of drawings that the jury or entrant might qualify as informal, including experimental and exploratory drawings, abstract works, collages, and anything else that one might consider to be "informal."

To fully appreciate the artwork reproduced on these pages, there is really no substitute for seeing the exhibition in person. In this catalogue, you will find a list of venues which, although complete at press time, is prone to changes and additions. You are encouraged to call ASAP for current information concerning AIP 11 and future shows.

Advanced Media Design
14 Imperial Place, Suite 202B
Providence, RI 02903
401-272-1637

Greater Buffalo International Airport
Greater Buffalo International Airport Design Group

Formal Category
Computer-generated, 12 x 20, 1995

Keiko Akasaka
Studio ARG
741-908 Iwagami-cho
Iwagami Rokkaku sagaru
Nakagyo-ku Kyoto 604
Japan
81-75-802-2291

T Project Atrium
RUI Architect & Associates, Osaka, Japan

Formal Category
Watercolor and airbrush, 17 x 23, 1994

Jim Anderson
Anderson Illustration Associates
1435 East Main Street
Madison, WI 53703
608-251-2025

SAUDI-ARAMCO Administrative Center
Sasaki Associates

Formal Category
Color pencil over black pencil, 17 x 27, 1994

Sachiko Asai
563 Ishiyama Minami-ku
Sapporo-shi Hokkaido 005
Japan
81-11-591-1683

Muroran Submarine Tunnel
Kitanihon Kouwan Port Consultant Company, Ltd., Japan

Formal Category
Watercolor, 1996

Luis Blanc
30 St. Felix Street #3A
Brooklyn, NY 11217
718-797-1267

Weiner Residence
David Weiner Architects, NY

Formal Category
Watercolor and wax pencil on illustration board, 10 x 24, 1995

Lori Brown
Lori Brown Consultants Ltd.
1639 West 2nd Avenue, Suite 410
Vancouver BC V6J 1H3
Canada
604-736-7897

Amanpuri—Place of Peace
Busby / Bridger Architects / Lori Brown

Formal Category
Pen and ink, 17 x 19, revised 1995

Frank M. Costantino
F.M. Costantino, Inc
13B Pauline Street
Winthrop, MA 02152
617-846-4766

Atlanta Braves Baseball Stadium
Atlanta Stadium Design Team

Formal Category
Color pencil on Mylar, 11 x 22, 1995

Elizabeth Ann Day
Elizabeth Day Architectural Illustration
1218 Baylor Street, Suite 204
Austin, TX 78703
512-469-6011

Holden Bridge
Burgess & Niple Engineers

Formal Category
Watercolor, 17 x 22, 1993

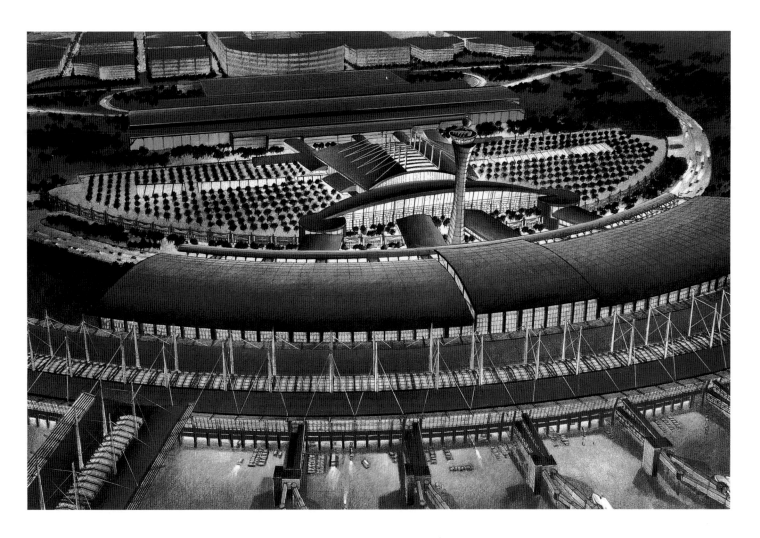

Stanley E. Doctor
747 Poplar Avenue
Boulder, CO 80304
303-449-3259

Transportation Center, Seoul Metropolitan Airport
Kaplan, McLaughlan, Diaz, San Francisco, CA

Formal Category
Color pencil, 21 x 32, 1995

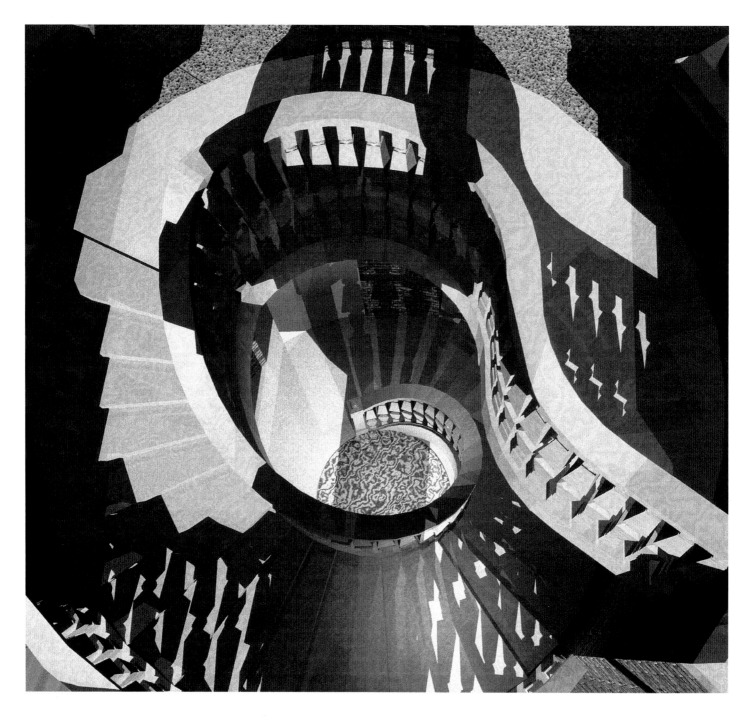

Lee Dunnette AIA
430 East 20th Street, 5B
New York, NY 10009
212-260-4240

Spiral Stair Interior
Self-commissioned

Formal Category
Computer rendering, 16 x 18, 1995

Jeffrey Michael George
Jeffrey Michael George Architectural Illustration
1800 Pacific Avenue #108
San Francisco, CA 94109
415-346-6621

Jose Theater
Redevelopment Agency of the City of San Jose

Formal Category
Color pencil and pastel, 19 x 28, 1994

Gilbert Gorski AIA

Gorski & Associates, P.C.
6633 Spokane Avenue
Lincolnwood, IL 60646
847-329-1340

Philadelphia Retail Center
Ellerbe Becket, Santa Monica, CA

Formal Category
Colored pencil and airbrush, 16 x 13, 1995

Christopher Grubbs
Christopher Grubbs Illustrator
601 4th Street Loft #112
San Francisco, CA 94107
415-243-4394

Obyan Beach Resort, Entry View
Hornberger & Worstell, San Francisco, CA

Formal Category
Prismacolor on color Xerox, 9 x 11, 1995

Douglas E. Jamieson

827 1/2 Via de la Paz
Pacific Palisades, CA 90272
310-573-1155

Teltow Housing
Zeidler Roberts Partners

Formal Category
Watercolor over pencil, 6 x 9, 1994

Marc D. L'Italien

L'Italien Architecture + Design
3740 25th Street, Suite 401
San Francisco, CA 94110
415-285-9062

Packing Tower / Slide Silo
The Architectural League of New York

Formal Category
Color pencil on vellum, 12 x 36, 1992

Peter Allen Landeck
606 West 49th Terrace
Kansas City, MO 64112
816-753-8855

Imaginary Bridge
Self-commissioned

Formal Category
Computer-generated, 30 x 40, 1996

Laura Clayton Linn
Hellmuth, Obata + Kassabaum
One Metropolitan Square, Suite 600
211 North Broadway
St. Louis, MO 63102-2733
314-421-2000

St. Louis Museum of Natural History
Gyo Obata, Elysse Newman

Formal Category
Watercolor, 10 x 10, 1995

James B. McBurney
1429 East River Road
Minneapolis, MN 55414
612-338-3014

Basilica Renovation at Conception Abbey
Rafferty Rafferty Tollefson Architects, Inc.

Formal Category
Gouache, colored pencil and ink, 29 x 23, 1991

Loek Meenhorst
Loek Meenhorst Visuals
Stadhuisplein 16C Almere
Holland
31-36-5336-449

Hirch Gebouw
Hirch Development

Formal Category
20 x 40

Michael B. Morrissey

Michael B. Morrissey & Company
223 Indian Road Crescent
Toronto ONT M6P 2G6
Canada
416-763-1387

Holderbank Consulting Ltd., Entry Facade
Dunlop Farrow Architects

Formal Category
Watercolor, 5 x 11, 1994

Mark S.C. Nelson AIA
Nelson Design
3205 South Maple Avenue
Berwyn, IL 60402
708-484-2720

Four Stamford Plaza Lobby ISI
Michael B. Morrissey & Company

Formal Category
Digital mapping and modeling, 21 x 28, 1995

J. Paul Newton
Parsons Brinckerhoff
1660 Lincoln Street, Suite 2000
Denver, CO 80264
303-832-9097

Miller Highway
Empire State Development

Formal Category
Computer (3D model and paint rendering), 1995

Martin J. Newton
Archimation
Kantstr.142, Berlin 10623
Germany
49-30-312-1306

Bahnhof Papestrasse
JSK / Perkins & Will

Formal Category
Computer-generated, 36 x 36, 1995

David S. Nobles

Impulse Images & Animations, Inc.
9310 Autumn Sunrise
San Antonio, TX 78250
210-521-7221

The Collective
David Nobles & Ken Frazier

Formal Category
Computer, 54 x 27, 1994

WAMPLER HALL
JAMES MADISON UNIVERSITY

Wesley L. Page AIA
Hanbury Evans Newill Vlattas & Company
120 Atlantic Street, Suite 400
Norfolk, VA 23510
804-627-5775

Wampler Hall, James Madison University
Hanbury Evans Newill Vlattas & Company

Formal Category
Gouache and colored pencil, 29 x 21, 1992

43

Stephen Parker, Associate AIA

802 Kipling Way
St. Charles, MO 63304
314-441-8370

Federal Reserve Bank of Cleveland
Steve Brubaker

Formal Category
Prismacolor pencil, 18 x 23, 1995

Michael Reardon
5433 Boyd Avenue
Oakland, CA 94618
510-655-7030

Bangkok International Airport
Hellmuth, Obata + Kassabaum, San Francisco

Formal Category
Pencil, 10 x 15, 1994

Thomas Wells Schaller AIA
Schaller Architectural Illustration
2112 Broadway, Suite 407
New York, NY 10023
212-362-5524

Friedrichstadt Q206, Berlin
Pei Cobb Freed & Partners

Formal Category
Watercolor and pencil, 18 x 24, 1995

Hideo Shirai
Shirai Pers House
31-8-213 Honcho
Wako-shi, Saitama-ken 351-01
Japan
81-48-465-1615

Miyagi Arena
Taisei Corporation, Japan

Formal Category
Airbrush, pen and ink, 500 x 700mm, 1994

James C. Smith
The Studio of James C. Smith
700 South Clinton Street, Suite 100
Chicago, IL 60607
312-987-0132

Saint Ignatius 1895
Toussaint Menard

Formal Category
Mixed media, 20 x 29, 1995

Dick Sneary
Sneary Architectural Illustration
9728 Overhill Road
Kansas City, MO 64134
816-765-7841

New York Life Building Restoration
Gastinger, Walker, Harden Architects

Formal Category
Watercolor, 10 x 8, 1995

Mohammed Saleh Uddin
1123 Woodhue Drive
Baton Rouge, LA 70810
504-767-3041

Rahman Residence
Self-commissioned

Formal Category
Composite photo and computer drawings

Koji Watanabe
Takenaka Corporation
4-1-13, Hommachi Chuoh-ku
Osaka 541
Japan
81-6-252-1201

Hansin Electric Railway Company
Takenaka Corporation

Formal Category
Watercolor, 21 x 27, 1995

Wendy Louise White
Robert McIlhargey & Associates, LTD
1639 West 2nd Avenue, Suite 410, Vancouver, BC V6J 1H3
Canada
604-731-7897

Avila At Waterfront Place, Vancouver
Perkins and Company

Formal Category
Mixed media, 29 x 19, 1995

Windtunnel Imaging & Animation
James Akers
560 Broadway, Suite 607
New York, NY 10012
212-274-1741

Kuala Lumpur City Center Atrium
Cesar Pelli / Walker Group-CNI

Formal Category
Digital image, 30 x 20, 1995

Curtis James Woodhouse
4141 Lybyer Avenue
Miami, FL 33133
305-663-8347

Forty-Second Street Theaters
Rockwell Architecture

Formal Category
Watercolor, 14 x 20, 1995

Tamotsu Yamamoto ASAP
15 Sleeper Street
Boston, MA 02210
617-542-1021

Kuwait Desert Storm Memorial Competition
HDS & Gallagher Inc., Boston

Formal Category
Watercolor, 22 x 30, 1993

Jerry Yin
NBBJ
111 South Jackson Street
Seattle, WA 98104
206-223-5168

Tulalip Cultural Museum
Tulalip Tribe

Formal Category
Color pencil, 15 x 30, 1995

Andrzej Zarzycki
41 Gorham Street
Somerville, MA 02144
617-776-3472

Facade Study for Ambulatory Speciality Center
TRO/The Richie Organization

Formal Category
Computer graphics, 8 x 10, 1995

Giang Dinh
7403 Franklin Road
Annandale, VA 22003
703-849-8610

Marc Chagall Museum in the Eye of a Dream Walker
Self-commissioned

Sketch Category
Oil on canvas, 20 x 42, 1993

WINDOWS & FRAGMENTS

Richard B. Ferrier FAIA

Firm X Architects
1628 Connally Terrace
Arlington, TX 76010
817-469-8605

Windows & Fragments = Memory & Desire
Self-commissioned

Sketch Category
Watercolor, photoimages, metals, graphite, 22 x 30, 1994

Stephan Hoffpauir AIA

640 Walavista Avenue

Oakland, CA 94610

510-272-9794

Electrical Power Station

Antonio Sant'Elia

Sketch Category

Watercolor and ink, 16 x 10, 1995

Ronald J. Love
Ronald J. Love Architectural Illustration
3891 Bayridge Avenue
West Vancouver BC V7V 3J3
Canada
604-922-3033

Art Museum
Self-commissioned

Sketch Category
Mixed media, 7 x 12, 1994

Barbara Worth Ratner AIA
828 Charles Allen Drive, NE
Atlanta, GA 30308
404-876-3943

Manufacturing Related Disciplines complex, Georgia Institute of Technology
Lord, Aeck and Sargent, Architects

Sketch Category
Watercolor on computer-generated line drawing, 8 x 28, 1994

Rael D. Slutsky AIA

Rael D. Slutsky & Associates, Inc.
351 Milford Road
Deerfield, IL 60015
847-267-8200

Chicago Music and Dance Theater
Hammond, Beeby, Babka

Sketch Category
Felt-tip pen, pastel, color pencil, 9 x 12, 1994

Stanislaw W. Szroborz

Atelier Szroborz
Merowingerstr. 120
Dusseldorf 40225
Germany
49-211-317-9693

City Carre Magdeburg
RKW Architects, Dusseldorf

Sketch Category
Mixed media, 20 x 30, 1995

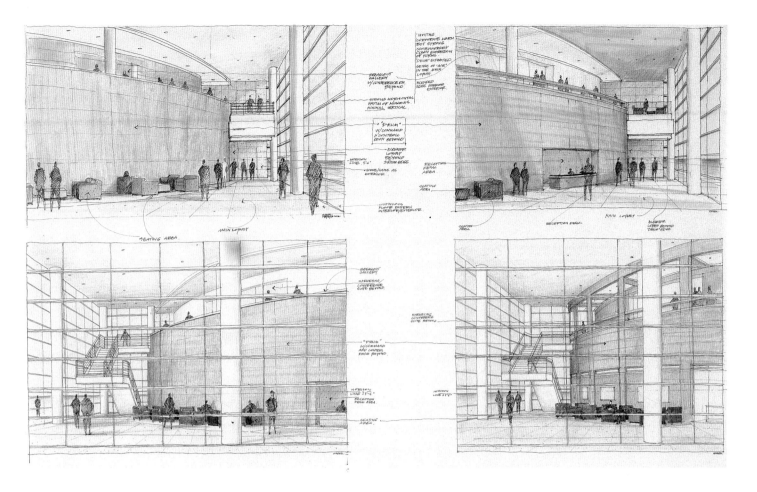

Marek Tryzybowicz

Hellmuth, Obata + Kassabaum, Inc.
6688 North Central Expressway, Suite 700
Dallas, TX 75206
214-739-6688

A Global Network Monitoring Facility, Lobby Studies
Hellmuth, Obata + Kassabaum, Inc.

Sketch Category
Pen, markers, color pencils, 18 x 24, 1995

For the first time this year, the jury members were asked to evaluate the works which were not selected for the traveling exhibition. On the following pages are the submitted works that the jury deemed exceptional enough to merit publication in the catalogue.

Advanced Media Design a
14 Imperial Place, Suite 202B
Providence, RI 02903
401-272-1637

Advanced Media Design b
14 Imperial Place, Suite 202B
Providence, RI 02903
401-272-1637

Keiko Akasaka c
Studio ARG
741-908 Iwagami-cho
Iwagami Rokkaku sagaru
Nakagyo-ku, Kyoto 604
Japan
81-75-802-2291

a

c

b

b

James Akers a
Akers Visualization
20 Prospect Street
Summit, NJ 07901
908-277-1909

Jim Anderson b
Anderson Illustration Associates
1435 East Main Street
Madison, WI 53703
608-251-2025

Yutaka Aoki c
707 NK Kojimachi Quarters
7-10 Sanbacho Chiyoda-ku, Tokyo 102
Japan
81-3-3263-4813

Sachiko Asai d
563 Ishiyama Minami-ku
Sapporo-shi, Hokkaido 005
Japan
81-11-591-1683

Richard C. Baehr AIA e
Architectural Rendering
305 Northern Boulevard
Great Neck, NY 11021
516-466-0470

a

c

d

e

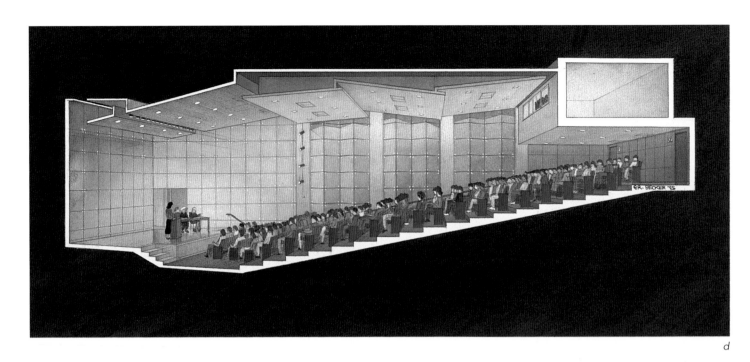

d

Richard C. Baehr AIA *a*
Architectural Rendering
305 Northern Boulevard
Great Neck, NY 11021
516-466-0470

Alexander Ballings *b*
7Arts Visuals
Mechtildisstraat 2
Tilburg 5021
Holland
31-13-535-53-41

Alexander Ballings *c*
7Arts Visuals
Mechtildisstraat 2
Tilburg 5021CN
Holland
31-13-535-53-41

Robert Becker *d*
2337 Balboa Street
San Francisco, CA 94121
415-752-9946

Susan M. Biasiolli AIA *e*
Kovert-Hawkins Architects
630 Walnut Street
Jeffersonville, IN 47130
812-282-9554

c

a

b

e

b

Anita S. Bice *a*
1009 Park Avenue
Moody, AL 35004
205-640-6168

Mohammed U. Bilbeisi AIA *b*
2022 West University Avenue
Stillwater, OK 74074
405-377-4748

Luis Blanc *c*
30 St. Felix Street #3A
Brooklyn, NY 11217
718-797-1267

Lori Brown *d*
Lori Brown Consultants Ltd.
1639 West 2nd Avenue, Suite 410
Vancouver BC V6J 1H3
Canada
604-736-7897

Nicholas Joel Buccalo *e*
The Drawing Studio
211 Warren Street
Brooklyn, NY 11201
718-488-7894

a

e

d

c

b

John S.M. Chen AIA *a*
12505 Montclair Drive
Silver Spring, MD 20904
301-680-0015

Richard Chenoweth AIA *b*
Architectural Watercolors
518 Margaret Drive
Silver Spring, MD 20910
301-588-0528

Mike Ciemny *c*
35-25 77th Street, B25
Jackson Heights, NY 11372
718-457-0965

Frank M. Costantino *d*
F.M. Costantino, Inc.
13B Pauline Street
Winthrop, MA 02152
617-846-4766

Frank M. Costantino *e*
F.M. Costantino, Inc.
13B Pauline Street
Winthrop, MA 02152
617-846-4766

e

c

d

a

b

Sandy Cuncu-McKinnon *a*
Robert McIlhargey and Associates, Ltd.
1639 West 2nd Avenue, Suite 410
Vancouver BC V6J 1H3
Canada
604-736-7897

Elizabeth Ann Day *b*
Elizabeth Day Architectural Illustration
1218 Baylor Street, Suite 204
Austin, TX 78703
512-469-6011

Elizabeth Ann Day *c*
Elizabeth Day Architectural Illustration
1218 Baylor Street, Suite 204
Austin, TX 78703
512-469-6011

Angelo DeCastro *d*
Rua Do Alto Da Milha, 50 A
Sao Joao Do Estoril 2765
Portugal
351-1-4671010

Angelo DeCastro *e*
Rua Do Alto Da Milha, 50 A
Sao Joao Do Estoril 2765
Portugal
351-1-4671010

a

c

d

e

e

Emmanuel R. DeGuzman *a*

Noni Architectural Perspectives
1531 Delmar Avenue
Kissimmee, FL 34744
407-933-5219

Rafael De Jesus *b*

306, 229-11 Avenue SE
Calgary ALB T2G OY1
Canada
403-265-3304

Edgardo A. de Lara *c*

Hellmuth, Obata + Kassabaum
6688 North Central Expressway, Suite 700
Dallas, TX 75206
214-739-6688

Robert I. Denmarsh *d*

309 Sleepy Hollow Road
Pittsburgh, PA 15228
412-561-2689

Wilson B. Deomampo *e*

18-05 Sherwood Towers
3 Jalan Anak Bukit 588988
Singapore
65-462-2358

b

c

d

a

b

Kenneth DiVito a
4347 Devonshire Drive
Troy, MI 48098
810-952-5155

Giang Dinh b
7403 Franklin Road
Annandale, VA 22003
703-849-8610

Stanley E. Doctor c
747 Poplar Avenue
Boulder, CO 80304
303-449-3259

Wei Dong d
1300 Linden Drive
Madison, WI 53706
608-262-8805

Lee A. Dunnette AIA e
430 East 20th Street, 5B
New York, NY 10009
212-260-4240

c

d

a

e

e

Lee A. Dunnette AIA a
430 East 20th Street, 5B
New York, NY 10009
212-260-4240

Michael M. Dwyer AIA b
Butterick, White & Burtis
475 Tenth Avenue, 7th floor
New York, NY 10018
212-967-3333

James F. Earl c
earl design
17 Parkview Drive
Hingham, MA 02043
617-749-7982

James F. Earl d
earl design
17 Parkview Drive
Hingham, MA 02043
617-749-7982

Peter R. Edgeley FSAI, RIBA e
Peter Edgeley PTY LTD
30 Queens Road, Suite 17
Melbourne Victoria 3004
Australia
613-9866-6620

a

d

b

c

a

Peter R. Edgeley FSAI, RIBA *a*

Peter Edgeley PTY LTD
30 Queens Road, Suite 17
Melbourne Victoria 3004
Australia
613-9866-6620

Bill Evans *b*

Presentations II
714 1st Avenue West
Seattle, WA 98119
206-282-8785

Craig D. Farnsworth *c*

Johnson, Johnson and Roy
30 West Monroe Street, Suite 1010
Chicago, IL 60603
312-641-0770

Richard B. Ferrier FAIA *d*

Firm X Architects
1628 Connally Terrace
Arlington, TX 76010
817-469-8605

Dudley M. Fleming *e*

Rockwood Sumner Grant
136 1/2 South Main Street Studio 1
Bowling Green, OH 43402
419-352-4740

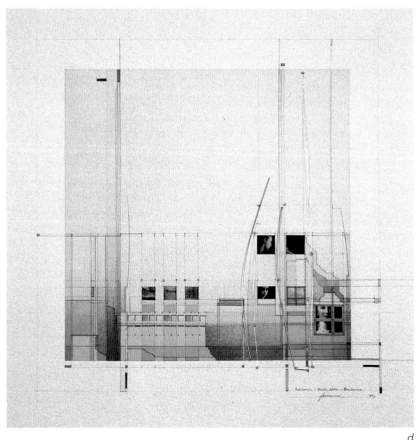

d

PEDESTRIAN VIEW OF
ATHLETIC SUPPORT BUILDING
LOYOLA UNIVERSITY CHICAGO
ATHLETIC FACILITIES DEVELOPMENT CONCEPTS

c

b

e

d

Jeffrey Michael George *a*

Jeffrey Michael George Architectural Illustration
1800 Pacific Avenue #108
San Francisco, CA 94109
415-346-6621

Oscar S. Glottmann *b*

Glottmann Architectural Corporation
317 Minorca Avenue #110
Coral Gables, FL 33134
305-446-8001

Gilbert Gorski AIA *c*

Gorski & Associates, P.C.
6633 Spokane Avenue
Lincolnwood, IL 60646
847-329-1340

Jane Grealy & Associates PTY LTD *d*

7/322 Old Cleveland Road
Coorparoo Brisbane Qld. 4151
Australia
617-3394-4333

Gordon Grice OAA, MRAIC *e*

35 Church Street Apt. 205
Toronto ONT M5E 1T3
Canada
416-536-9191

b

c

a

e

a

Gordon Grice OAA, MRAIC *a*
35 Church Street #205
Toronto ONT M5E 1T3
Canada
416-536-9191

Christopher Grubbs Illustrator *b*
601 4th Street Loft #112
San Francisco, CA 94107
415-243-4394

Christopher Grubbs Illustrator *c*
601 4th Street Loft #112
San Francisco, CA 94107
415-243-4394

A. Melissa Harris RA *d*
University of Michigan
College of Architecture & Urban Planning
2000 Bonisteel Blvd.
Ann Arbor, MI 48109
313-936-0224

John A. Hawkins AIA *e*
Creative Design Illustrations
630 Walnut Street
Jeffersonville, IN 47130
812-282-9554

b

c

e

d

e

John A. Hawkins AIA *a*
Creative Design Illustrations
630 Walnut Street
Jeffersonville, IN 47130
812-282-9554

Tomomi Hayashi *b*
Shimizubunka
2-130 Higashisonoda-cho
Amagasaki Hyogo 661
Japan
81-6-498-5735

Andy Hickes *c*
205 Third Avenue #98
New York, NY 10003
212-677-8054

Stephan Hoffpauir *d*
640 Walavista Avenue
Oakland, CA 94610
510-272-9794

William G. Hook *e*
1501 Western Avenue, Suite 500A
Seattle, WA 98101
206-622-3849

a

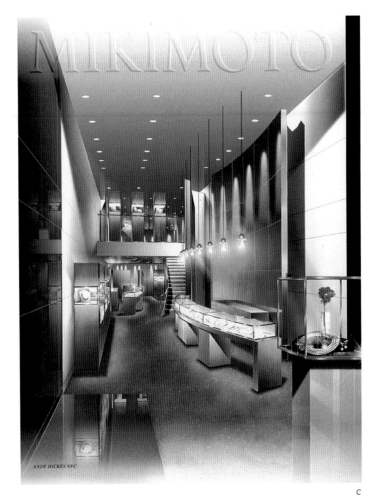

b

c

d

d

William G. Hook *a*
1501 Western Avenue, Suite 500A
Seattle, WA 98101
206-622-3849

Howard R. Huizing *b*
145 South Olive Street
Orange, CA 92666
714-532-3012

Howard R. Huizing *c*
145 South Olive Street
Orange, CA 92666
714-532-3012

Suns Hung *d*
Sun Associate Arts & Design
445 Fifth Avenue, Suite 19F
New York, NY 10016
212-779-4977

Suns Hung *e*
Sun Associate Arts & Design
445 Fifth Avenue, Suite 19F
New York, NY 10016
212-779-4977

a

e

c

b

CHUÔ-LINE NEW PROJECT

b

Eric Hyne *a*
Encore Arts
5256 Buchanan Trail East, Suite 104
Waynesboro, PA 17268
717-765-9233

Yoshie Ideno *b*
707 NK Kojimachi Quarters
7-10 Sanban-cho
Chiyoda-ku Tokyo102
Japan
81-3-3263-4813

Douglas E. Jamieson *c*
827 1/2 Via de la Paz
Pacific Palisades, CA 90272
310-573-1155

Douglas E. Jamieson *d*
827 1/2 Via de la Paz
Pacific Palisades, CA 90272
310-573-1155

Angelito Altares Jimenez *e*
26 Bacon Street, East Tapinac
Olongapo City, Subic Bay 2200
Philippines
6347-223-4051

e

c

d

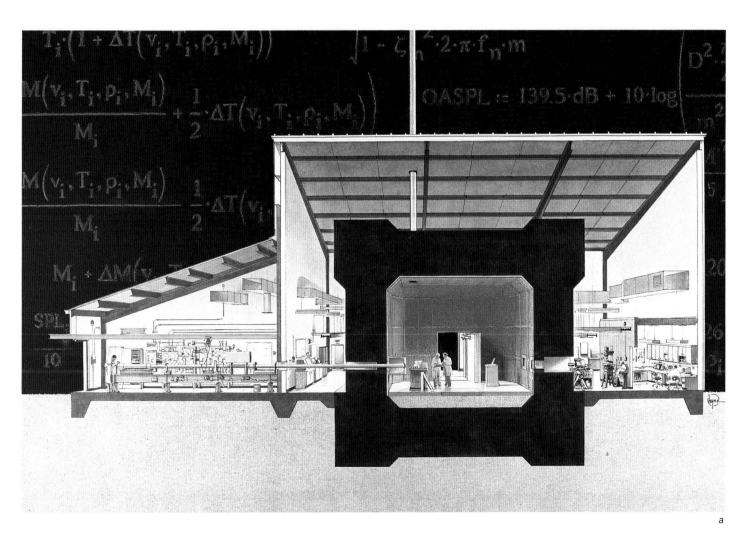

a

a

David E. Joyner *a*
Presentation Techniques
P.O. Box 11173
Knoxville, TN 37939-1173
423-584-8334

Takuji Kariya *b*
1-5-5-406 Tomobuchi-cho
Miyakojima-ku Osaka 534
Japan
81-6-924-3637

Choong-Jin Kim *c*
Room #505 (Pusan Dept)
1-1, Dong Kwang-Dong Jung-Ku
Pusan 600-021
South Korea
82-51-245-7333

Joseph C. Knight *d*
Knight Architects
4660 Village Court
Dunwoody, GA 30338
770-349-2798

Hisào Konishi *e*
741-908 Iwagami-cho
Iwagamidori Rokkaku Sagaru
Nakagyo-ku, Kyoto 604
Japan
81-75-802-2291

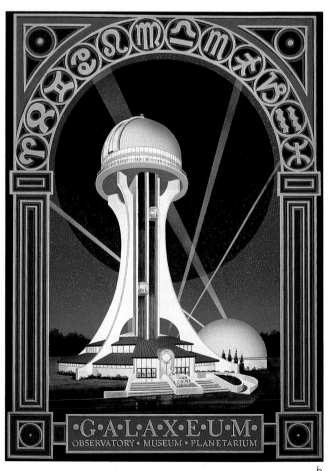

b

c

d

e

d

Yoshio Kono *a*
4 13, 3-Chome Kamirenjaku
Mitaka-shi, Tokyo 181
Japan
81-422-42-3795

Marc D. L'Italien *b*
L'Italien Architecture + Design
3740 25th Street, Suite 401
San Francisco, CA 94110
415-285-9062

Peter Allen Landeck *c*
606 West 49th Terrace
Kansas City, MO 64112
816-753-8855

Sun Ho Lee *d*
Suk Jun Bldg. #601
364-31 Seogko-Dong
Mapo-ku, Seoul
Korea
82-2-334-2118

Lawrence Ko Leong *e*
80027th Avenue
San Francisco, CA 94121
415-387-6528

b

a

c

e

a

Jens R. Lerback a
Architectural Illustrations
5414 SW Logan Court
Portland, OR 97219
503-452-1703

Wei Li b
11 Pine Knob Drive
Albany, NY 12203
518-431-3379

Laura Clayton Linn c
Hellmuth, Obata + Kassabaum
211 North Broadway, Suite 600
St. Louis, MO 63102-2733
314-421-2010x2476

George S. Loli d
116 St. Julien Avenue
Lafayette, LA 70506
318-232-3231

Ronald J. Love e
Ronald J. Love Architectural Illustration
3891 Bayridge Avenue
West Vancouver BC V7V 3J3
Canada
604-922-3033

c

e

b

d

c

Ronald J. Love a
Ronald J. Love Architectural Illustration
3891 Bayridge Avenue
West Vancouver, BC V7V 3J3
Canada
604-922-3033

Dr. Peter Magyar b
Spaceprint, Inc.
632 Beaumont Drive
State College, PA 16801
814-466-3054

George A. Marcincavage c
16 Beekman Place
Fair Lawn, NJ 07410
201-670-9200

John P. Margolis AIA d
Margolis, Inc.
380 Boylston Street
Boston, MA 02116
617-859-2950

Gretchen Maricak e
1040 Chapin
Birmingham, MI 48009
810-644-3001

a

b

e

d

b

Yasuko Matsuda *a*
5-21-6, Katsutadai
Yachiyo Chiba 276
Japan
81-474-83-8574

William A. McBride WAM *b*
Architectural Illustration
18 West 59th Street
Kansas City, MO 64113
816-523-2345

James B. McBurney *c*
1429 East River Road
Minneapolis, MN 55414
612-338-3014

Robert McIlhargey *d*
1639 West 2nd Avenue, Suite 410
Vancouver BC V6J 1H3
Canada
604-736-7897

Robert McIlhargey *e*
1639 West 2nd Avenue, Suite 410
Vancouver BC V6J 1H3
Canada
604-736-7897

c

d

a

e

a

Loek Meenhorst *a*
Loek Meenhorst Visuals
Stadhuisplein 16C Almere
Holland
31-36-5336-449

Ayako Mochizuki *b*
13-204 Nishiisya-danchi
1-19 Kamenoi, Meito-ku
Nagoya Aichi 465
Japan
81-52-701-4235

Michael B. Morrissey *c*
Michael B. Morrissey & Company
223 Indian Road Crescent
Toronto ONT M6P 2G6
Canada
416-763-1387

Mark S.C. Nelson AIA *d*
Nelson Design
3205 South Maple Avenue
Berwyn, IL 60402-2809
708-484-2730

Martin J. Newton *e*
Archimation
Kantstr.142, Berlin 10623
Germany
49-30-312-1306

b

d

c

e

a

J. Paul Newton *a*
Parsons Brinckerhoff
1660 Lincoln Street, Suite 2000
Denver, CO 80264
303-832-9097

David S. Nobles *b*
Impulse Images & Animations, Inc.
9310 Autumn Sunrise
San Antonio, TX 78250
210-521-7221

Michko Nojima *c*
Kosumo Kameido Bunka 205
17-12 Chome Bunka
Sumida-ku Tokyo 131
Japan
81-3-3616-1287

Don Oelfke, Jr. *d*
Don Oelfke Design
P.O. Box 163746
Austin, TX 78716-3746
512-328-3381

Paul Stevenson Oles FAIA *e*
Interface Architects
One Gateway Center, Suite 501 A
Newton, MA 02158
617-527-6790

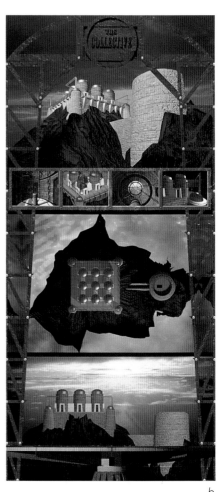

b

c

d

e

b

Orest Associates *a*
3757 Main Highway
P.O. Box 809
Miami, FL 33133
305-446-8159

Paul B. Ostergaard AIA *b*
UDA Architects
113 Pennsylvania Avenue
Pittsburgh, PA 15222
412-765-1133

Wesley L. Page AIA *c*
Hanbury Evans Newill Vlattas & Company
120 Atlantic Street, Suite 400
Norfolk, VA 23510
804-627-5775

Stephen Parker, Associate AIA *d*
802 Kipling Way
St. Charles, MO 63304
314-441-8370

Gang Peng *e*
78 Sycamore Street #2
Somerville, MA 02145
617-666-6014

a

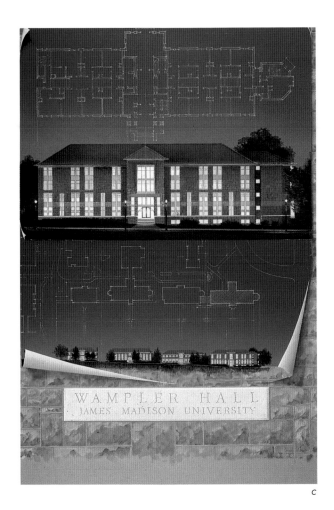

c

d

e

b

c

Merike B. Phillips a
M. Phillips Architectural Illustration
711 61st Street
Kenosha, WI 53143
414-658-8464

Eugene V. Radvenis b
E.V. Radvenis, Inc.
1639 West 2nd Avenue, Suite 410
Vancouver BC V6J 1H3
Canada
604-736-5430

Eugene V. Radvenis c
E.V. Radvenis, Inc.
1639 West 2nd Avenue, Suite 410
Vancouver BC V6J 1H3
Canada
604-736-5430

Barbara Worth Ratner AIA d
828 Charles Allen Drive, NE
Atlanta, GA 30308
404-876-3943

Michael Reardon e
5433 Boyd Avenue
Oakland, CA 94618
510-655-7030

d

a

e

a

Eamon Regan a

Sutton Yantis Associates Architects
1952 Gallows Road Suite 100
Vienna, VA 22182
703-734-9733

Travis Rice b

Crose-Gardner Associates, Inc.
414 61st Street
Des Moines, IA 50312
515-274-4925

Samuel C. Ringman c

Ringman Design and Illustration
1800 McKinney Avenue
Dallas, TX 75201
214-871-9001

Al Rusch AIA d

Phillips Swager Associates
3622 North Knoxville Avenue
Peoria, IL 61603
309-688-9511

Sakal and Hood e

1012 Colley Avenue
Norfolk, VA 23507
804-622-6991

c

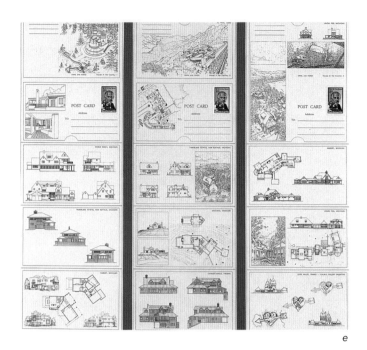

e

d

b

d

Philip Sampson a
Leo A. Daly
8600 Indian Hills Drive
Omaha, NE 68114
402-391-8111

Philip Sampson b
Leo A. Daly
8600 Indian Hills Drive
Omaha, NE 68114
402-391-8111

Thomas Wells Schaller AIA c
Schaller Architectural Illustration
2112 Broadway, Suite 407
New York, NY 10023
212-362-5524

Thomas Wells Schaller AIA d
Schaller Architectural Illustration
2112 Broadway, Suite 407
New York, NY 10023
212-362-5524

Eric C. Schleef e
Eric Schleef Illustration
7740 Dean Road
Indianapolis, IN 46240
317-595-0016

b

c

a

e

e

Thomas A. Schmidt *a*
1020 Green Street #104
Honolulu, HI 96822
808-524-5524

George A. Schneider *b*
Watercolors by Schneider
804 South Fifth Street
Columbus, OH 43206
614-443-7014

Thomas G. Sherrill *c*
Caperton-Johnson, Inc.
14860 Montfort, Suite 200
Dallas, TX 75240
214-991-7082

Kazuko Shimada *d*
7-3-4-404 Hikarigaoka
Nerima-ku Tokyo179
Japan
81-3-3939-8522

Hideo Shirai *e*
Shirai Pers House
31-8-213 Honcho
Wako-shi, Saitama-ken 351-01
Japan
81-48-465-1615

b

d

c

a

a

Hisae Shoda *a*
Takenaka Corporation
8-24-305, 2 Chome Deguchi
Hirakata-shi, Osaka 573
Japan
81-720-35-2690

Rael D. Slutsky AIA *b*
Rael D. Slutsky & Associates, Inc.
351 Milford Road
Deerfield, IL 60015
847-267-8200

James C. Smith *c*
The Studio of James C. Smith
700 South Clinton Street, Suite 100
Chicago, IL 60607
312-987-0132

Dick Sneary *d*
Sneary Architectural Illustration
9728 Overhill Road
Kansas City, MO 64134
816-765-7841

Henry Sorenson *e*
702 South 14th Avenue
Bozeman, MT 59715
406-587-7113

c

d

b

e

a

Kenneth Stuart *a*
The Larson Company
6701 South Midvale Park Road
Tucson, AZ 85746
520-294-3900

Stanislaw W. Szroborz *b*
Atelier Szroborz
Merowingerstr. 120
Dusseldorf 40225
Germany
49-211-317-9693

Dario Tainer AIA *c*
Tainer Associates, Ltd.
445 West Erie Street
Chicago, IL 60610
312-951-1656

Masakazu Takahata *d*
1-38-21 Kuzuha Noda
Hirakata-shi
Osaka 573
Japan
81-720-57-4044

Masakazu Takahata *e*
1-38-21 Kuzuha Noda
Hirakata-shi
Osaka 573
Japan
81-720-57-4044

d

b

c

e

d

Mongkol Tansantisuk AIA *a*
Architectural Presentations
672 Grove Street
Newton, MA 02162-1319
617-332-7885

Mongkol Tansantisuk AIA *b*
Architectural Presentations
672 Grove Street
Newton, MA 02162-1319
617-332-7885

Sergei E. Tchoban *c*
NBS & Partner
Ulmenstr. 40
Hamburg 22299
Germany
49-40-4806180

Rene Thibault *d*
407-1509 Centre Street SW
Calgary ALB T2G 2E6
Canada
403-262-4383

Kevin Triplett *e*
79 Phillips Lane
Wrentham, MA 02093
617-423-1700

c

b

a

e

c

Marek Tryzybowicz *a*
Hellmuth, Obata + Kassabaum, Inc.
6688 North Central Expressway, Suite 700
Dallas, TX 75206
214-739-6688

Mohammed Saleh Uddin *b*
1123 Woodhue Drive
Baton Rouge, LA 70810
504-767-3041

Mark Ueland AIA *c*
Ueland, Junker & McCauley, Architects
718 Arch Street, 5th Floor
Philadelphia, PA 19106
215-440-0190

Willem van den Hoed *d*
1000 Huizen
Lange Geer 44, Delft 2611 PW
The Netherlands
31-1521-33382

Evan Visser *e*
3050 Gold Dust NE
Belmont, MI 49306
616-676-0890

b

d

a

e

e

Masanari Wakita JARA *a*
Takenaka Corporation
1-26 Higashiyamamoto-machi
Chikusa-ku
Nagoya Aichi 464
Japan
81-52-781-4474

Koji Watanabe *b*
2-20-3, Ibukino
Izumi-shi, Osaka 594
Japan
81-725-56-7608

Andrew S. K. Wee *c*
453 Upper East Coast Road
#03-03 The Summit 466501
Singapore
4423115/258866

Wendy Louise White *d*
Robert McIlhargey & Associates, Ltd.
1639 West 2nd Avenue, Suite 410
Vancouver BC V6J 1H3
Canada
604-731-7897

Daniel E. Willis AIA *e*
1921 North Oak Lane
State College, PA 16803
814-867-5459

d

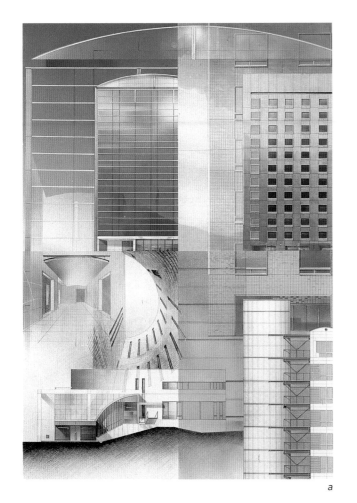

a

b

c

a

Windtunnel Imaging & Animation a
James Akers
560 Broadway, Suite 607
New York, NY 10012
212-274-1741

Max Gandi Wolf b
2936 Morcom Avenue
Oakland, CA 94619
510-536-9850

Curtis James Woodhouse c
4141 Lybyer Avenue
Miami, FL 33133
305-663-8347

Curtis James Woodhouse d
4141 Lybyer Avenue
Miami, FL 33133
305-663-8347

Masaaki Yamada e
Nikken Sekkei
1-4-27 Koraku Bunkyo-ku
Tokyo 112
Japan
81-3-3813-3361

b

c

d

e

d

Masaaki Yamada *a*
Nikken Sekkei
1-4-27 Koraku Bunkyo-ku
Tokyo 112
Japan
81-3-3813-3361

Tamotsu Yamamoto ASAP *b*
15 Sleeper Street
Boston, MA 02210
617-542-1021

Emiko Yanagida *c*
Hara Bldg., 4F
3-13-1 Hiroo Sibuya-ku
Tokyo 150
Japan
81-3-3400-0371

Zhengmao John Yang *d*
The Butner Architectural Group, P.C.
300 A Water Street, Suite 200
Montgomery, AL 36104
334-264-8888

Jerry Yin *e*
NBBJ
111 South Jackson Street
Seattle, WA 98104
206-223-5168

e

c

a

b

d

Fujio Yoshida a
301, 4-7-11 Zuiko
Higashi Yodogawa-ku, Osaka 533
Japan
81-6-327-4947

Kazunori Yoshimoto b
204 Fukuokachikuyu-ryo
1-2-3 Chuo
Onojo Fukuoka 816
Japan
81-92-593-9606

Tomoko Yoshimura c
21-27 Kunimatsu-cho
Neyagawa-shi, Osaka 572
Japan
81-720-22-2557

Roger Maolin Yu d
11 Progress Avenue, Suite 200
Scarborough ONT M1P 4S7
Canada
416-609-8418

Serge Zaleski FSAI, ARAIA e
Delineation Graphix
238 Bulwara Road
Ultimo, Sydney NSW 2007
Australia
61-2-552-3666

a

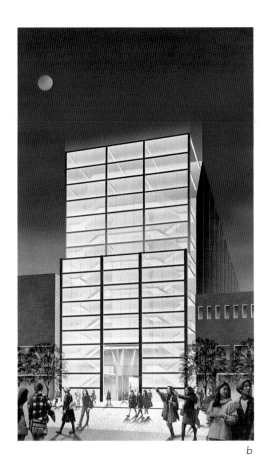

b

e

c

a

Andrzej Zarzycki *a*
41 Gorham Street
Somerville, MA 02144
617-776-3472

Arron K. Zimmerman *b*
W R S, Inc.
120 NW Parkway
Kansas City, MO 64150
816-587-9500

Partial East Elevation

b

Advanced Media Design
14 Imperial Place, Suite 202B
Providence, RI 02903
401-272-1637
Fax: 401-272-6240

Akasaka, Keiko
Studio ARG
741-908 Iwagami-cho
Iwagami Rokkaku sagaru
Nakagyo-ku, Kyoto 604
Japan
81-75-802-2291
Fax: 81-75-802-5117

Akers, James
Akers Visualization
20 Prospect Street
Summit, NJ 07901
908-277-1909
Fax: 908-277-0578

Alessi, Lawrence
72 Seminole
Pontiac, MI 48341

Anderson, Jim
Anderson Illustration Associates
1435 East Main Street
Madison, WI 53703
608-251-2025
Fax: 608-255-7750

Antwis, Donald
7 Arvon Street
Beachmere QLD 4510
Australia
61-74-968645
Fax: 61-74-968043

Aoki, Yutaka
707 NK Kojimachi Quarters
7-10 Sanbancho, Chiyoda-ku
Tokyo 102
Japan
81-3-3263-4813
Fax: 81-3-3263-5130

Archer, Melanie
Hampton Univ. Dept. of Architecture
Bemis Labs
Hampton, VA 23668

Asai, Sachiko
563 Ishiyama Minami-ku
Sapporo-shi Hokkaido 005
Japan
81-11-591-1683
Fax: 81-11-591-9519

Ashe, Chandana
380 West Hopkin
Pontiac, MI 48430

Baehr, Richard C., AIA
305 Northern Boulevard
Great Neck, NY 11021
516-466-0470
Fax: 516-466-1670

Ball, Daniel H.
239 West North Broadway
Columbus, OH 43214
614-478-2385
Fax: 614-478-3434

Ballings, Alexander
7Arts Visuals
Mechtildisstraat 2, Tilburg 5021 CN
Holland
31-13-535 53 41
Fax: 31-13-5364881

Barar, Valerie
2871 Troy Center Drive #2009
Troy, MI 48084

Bass, Dilian
Hampton Univ. Dept. of Architecture
Bemis Labs
Hampton, VA 23668

Becker, Robert
2337 Balboa Street
San Francisco, CA 94121
415-752-9946
Fax: 415-752-9947

Biasiolli, Susan M., AIA
Kovert-Hawkins Architects
630 Walnut Street
Jeffersonville, IN 47130
812-282-9554
Fax: 812-282-9171

Bice, Anita S.
1009 Park Avenue
Moody, AL 35004
205-640-6168
Fax: 205-640-6168

Bilbeisi, Mohammed U., AIA
2022 West University Avenue
Stillwater, OK 74074
405-377-4748
Fax: 405-377-3831

Blackman, Ed L.
Blackman Architectural Illustrations
180 NE 32nd Court
Fort Lauderdale, FL 33334

Blanc, Luis
30 St. Felix Street, 3A
Brooklyn, NY 11217
718-797-1267
Fax: 718-522-1511

Blye, Steven
3906 Gilbert Aenue
Western Springs, IL 60558
708-246-5040
Fax: 312-245-5255

Boyle, Kevin
575 East Troy Apt. #1
Ferndale, MI 48220

Brinson, David J., AIA
Brinson & Betts, AIA Architects
7948 Goodwood Boulevard
Baton Rouge, LA 70806
504-926-5045
Fax: 504-926-5046

Broland, Kathryn
88 Pendleton Lane
Londonderry, NH 03053
603-432-0736

Brown, Lori
Lori Brown Consultants Ltd.
1639 West 2nd Avenue, Suite 410
Vancouver BC V6J 1H3
Canada
604-736-7897
Fax: 604-736-9763

Brown, Stephen A.
110 Lakeview Avenue
Waltham, MA 02154
617-367-6300
Fax: 617-742-8722

Buccalo, Nicholas Joel
The Drawing Studio
211 Warren Street
Brooklyn, NY 11201
718-488-7894
Fax: 718-488-7894

Bunkley, Natalie
Hampton Univ. Dept. of Architecture
Bemis Labs
Hampton, VA 23668

Burroughs, Michael K.
14342 Sunrise Drive NE
Bainbridge Island, WA 98110
206-623-4646
Fax: 206-623-4625

Cermak, Dianne S.P.
The Book-Lined Room
34 Glendoon Road
Needham, MA 02192
617-455-6334
617-433-0839

Chao, Hans K.
101 Western Avenue #54
Cambridge, MA 02139
617-497-9924

Chen, John S.M., AIA
12505 Montclair Drive
Silver Spring, MD 20904
301-680-0015
Fax: 301-680-0756

Chenoweth, Richard, AIA
Architectural Watercolors
518 Margaret Drive
Silver Spring, MD 20910
301-588-0528
Fax: 301-589-0336

Church, Ron
21211 West Ten Mile Road #702
Southfield, MI 48075

Ciemny, Mike
35-25 77th Street B25
Jackson Heights, NY 11372
718-457-0965

Clement, Norma A., AIA
Lund Associates
1621 Sheridan Lake Road
Rapid City, SD 57702
605-348-3555
Fax: 605-348-6254

Coleman, Wesley
Hampton Univ. Dept. of Architecture
Bemis Labs
Hampton, VA 23668

Cooper, Keita
Hampton Univ. Dept. of Architecture
Bemis Labs
Hampton, VA 23668

Costantino, Frank M.
F.M. Costantino, Inc.
13B Pauline Street
Winthrop, MA 02152
617-846-4766
Fax: 617-846-4766

Cuncu-McKinnon, Sandra
Robert McIlhargey & Associates, Ltd.
1639 West 2nd Avenue, Suite 410
Vancouver BC V6J 1H3
Canada
604-736-7897
Fax: 604-736-9763

Dabrowska, Alina M.
822, 3130, 66 Ave SW
Calgary ALB T3E 5K8
Canada
403-249-7008

Davidge, Barney
Barney Davidge Associates
401 Alberto Way, Suite 5
Los Gatos, CA 95032
408-356-5634
Fax: 408-356-8688

Dawkins, Kenia
Hampton Univ. Dept. of Architecture
Bemis Labs
Hampton, VA 23668

Day, Elizabeth Ann
Elizabeth Day Architectural Illustration
1218 Baylor Street, Suite 204
Austin, TX 78703
512-469-6011
Fax: 512-469-6020

DeCastro, Angelo
Rua Do Alto Da Milha, 50A
Sao Joao Do Estoril 2765
Portugal
351-1-4671010
Fax: 351-1-4661648

De Jesus, Rafael
306, 229-11th Avenue SE
Calgary ALB T2G 0Y1
Canada
403-265-3304
Fax: 403-266-1992

de Lara, Edgardo A.
Hellmuth, Obata + Kassabaum
6688 North Central Expwy, Suite 700
Dallas, TX 75206
214-739-6688
Fax: 214-373-9523

DeGuzman, Emmanuel R.
Noni Architectural Perspectives
1531 Delmar Avenue
Kissimmee, FL 34744
407-933-5219
Fax: 407-933-5219

Denmarsh, Robert I.
309 Sleepy Hollow Road
Pittsburgh, PA 15228
412-561-2689

Deomampo, Wilson B.
18-05 Sherwood Towers
3 Jalan Anak Bukit 588988
Singapore
65-462-2358

Dickson, Nancy L.
7001 Jackson Drive
San Diego, CA 92119
619-558-6771

Dinh, Giang
7403 Franklin Road
Annandale, VA 22003
703-849-8610

DiVito, Kenneth
4347 Devonshire Drive
Troy, MI 48098
810-952-5155
Fax: 810-952-5155

Dixion, Raymond
Vanishing Point Illustrations
9317 Ingalls Street
Westminster, CO 80030
303-426-1202
Fax: 303-429-5113

Djohan, Ferry
JL.X(EKS) No.23 Rt.05/010
Kebonbaru Tebet, Jakarta 12830
Indonesia
62-21-828-0681
Fax: 62-21-828-0681

Do, Tung Th., AIA
GMB Architects & Engineers
PO Box 2159, 145 College Avenue
Holland, MI 49422-2159
616-392-7034
Fax: 616-392-2677

Doctor, Stanley E.
747 Poplar Avenue
Boulder, CO 80304
303-449-3259
Fax: 303-449-0629

Dong, Wei
1300 Linden Drive
Madison, WI 53706
608-262-8805
Fax: 608-262-5335

Dunnette, Lee A., AIA
430 East 20th Street, 5B
New York, NY 10009
212-260-4240
Fax: 212-353-2305

Dwyer, Michael M., AIA
Butterick, White & Burtis
475 Tenth Avenue, 7th Floor
New York, NY 10018
212-967-3333
Fax: 212-629-3749

Earl, James F.
Earl Design
17 Parkview Drive
Hingham, MA 02043
617-749-7982

Easton, John H.
1900 North Torrey Pines Drive #211
Las Vegas, NV 89108
702-229-6226
Fax: 702-382-3232

Edgeley, Peter R., FSAI, RIBA
Peter Edgeley PTY LTD
30 Queens Road, Suite 17
Melbourne Victoria 3004
Australia
613-9866-6620
Fax: 613-9866-6621

Elabd, Samir
Truex deGroot Collins Architects
209 Battery Street
Burlington, VT 05401
802-658-2775

Estor, Ramon A.
2140 East Hacienda Avenue
Las Vegas, NV 89119
702-798-1781

Evans, Bill
Presentations 11
714 1st Avenue West
Seattle, WA 98119
206-282-8785
Fax: 206-282-8784

Evans, George W.
6517 Shady Valley Drive
Flowery Branch, GA 30542
404-609-9330
Fax: 404-609-9308

Farnsworth, Craig D.
Johnson, Johnson and Roy
30 West Monroe Street, Suite 1010
Chicago, IL 60603
312-641-0770
Fax: 312-641-6728

Fernando, Pablo Claver
CICADA PVT. LTD.
1 Sophia Rd., 04-13 Peace Center
Singapore
65-334-7776
Fax: 65-297-3392

Ferrier, Richard B., FAIA
Firm X Architects
1628 Connally Terrace
Arlington, TX 76010
817-469-8605
Fax: 817-272-5098

Fleming, Dudley M.
Rockwood Sumner Grant
136 1/2 South Main St., Studio 1
Bowling Green, OH 43402
419-352-4740
Fax: 419-353-4576

Frank, Robert
Robert Frank Assoicates
2858 Sacramento Street
San Francisco, CA 94115
415-749-1418
Fax: 415-749-1418

Fritz, Steve
1815 East Front Street
Traverse City, MI 49686
616-947-3059
Fax: 616-947-7669

Frost, Jeff
3104 Gold Dust
Belmont, MI 49306

Garnett, Ronald L.
11635 Sedgemore Drive South
Jacksonville, FL 32223
904-791-4500
Fax: 904-791-4697

Genesis Studios Inc.
225 South Swoope Avenue #205
Maitland, FL 32751
407-539-2606
Fax: 407-644-7901

George, Jeffrey Michael
Jeffrey Michael George Architectural Illustration
1800 Pacific Avenue #108
San Francisco, CA 94109
415-346-6621
Fax: 415-346-5398

Gillam, James
James Gillam Architects
1841 Powell Street
San Francisco, CA 94133
415-398-1128
Fax: 415-398-1129

Gillette, Nathan
21211 West Ten Mile Road #905
Southfield, MI 48075

Glottmann, Oscar S.
Glottman Architectural Corporation
317 Minorca Avenue #110
Coral Gables, FL 33134
305-446-8001

Gohl, Roger
Roger Gohl Design Studio
2643 Stoner Avenue
Los Angeles, CA 90064
310-479-0754
Fax: 310-479-445

Gorman, Paul
801 79th Street #304
Darien, IL 60561
208-887-8483

Gorski, Gilbert, AIA
Gorski & Associates, P.C.
6633 Spokane Avenue
Lincolnwood, IL 60646
847-329-1340
Fax: 847-329-9321

Grealy, Jane
Jane Grealy & Associates PTY LTD
7/322 Old Cleveland Road
Coorparoo Brisbane Qld. 4151
Australia
617-3394-4333
Fax: 617-3849-0646

Grice, Gordon, OAA, MRAIC
35 Church Street Apt. 205
Toronto ONT M5E 1T3
Canada
416-536-9191
Fax: 416-696-8866

Grossi, Jason
2705 Jos. St. Louis Avenue
Windsor ONT N8T 2M7
Canada

Grubbs, Christopher A.
Christopher Grubbs Illustrator
601 Fourth Street Loft #112
San Francisco, CA 94107
415-243-4394
Fax: 415-243-4395

Haffey, Samuel A.
260 Fifth Avenue 2N
New York, NY 10001
212-725-5170
Fax: 212-689-5045

Hamersky, Bohdan C.
PO Box 204/41 Horne Tooke Road
Palisades, NY 10964
212-675-0400
Fax: 212-620-4687

Hanna, Jack
University of Houston Art Dept.
348 Fine Arts Building
Houston, TX 77204-4893
713-743-2831
Fax: 713-743-2823

Harmon, Dan U.
Dan Harmon & Associates
2089 McKinley Road NW
Atlanta, GA 30318
404-609-9330
Fax: 404-609-9308

Harris, Melissa A., RA
University of Michigan
College of Architecture & Urban Planning
2000 Bonisteel Blvd.
Ann Arbor, MI 48109
313-936-0224
Fax: 313-763-2322

Hart Linda M.
272 South Clark Drive
Beverly Hills, CA 90211-2609
310-854-5426
Fax: 310-854-5426

Hawkins, John A., AIA
630 Walnut Street
Jeffersonville, IN 47130
812-282-9554
Fax: 812-282-9171

Hayashi, Tomomi
Shimizubunka
2-130 Higashisonoda-cho
Amagasaki Hyogo 661
Japan
81-6-498-5735

Hickes, Andy
205 Third Avenue #98
New York, NY 10003
212-677-8054
Fax: 212-677-8054

Hoffpauir, Stephan, AIA
640 Walavista Avenue
Oakland, CA 94610
510-272-9794
Fax: 510-272-9794

Holly, Brent
37849 Lakeshore Drive
Harrison Twp., MI 48045
810-465-7912

Hood, Sallie A.
Sakal and Hood, Architects
1012 Colley Avenue
Norfolk, VA 23507
804-622-6991
Fax: 804-622-6991

Hook, William G.
1501 Western Avenue, Suite 500A
Seattle, WA 98101
206-622-3849
Fax: 206-624-1494

Howard, Dick
Howard Associates
5800 Monroe Street
Sylvania, OH 43560
419-882-7131
Fax: 419-882-8710

Huizing, Howard R.
145 South Olive Street
Orange, CA 92666
714-532-3012
Fax: 714-532-5298

Hung, Suns
Sun Associate Arts & Design
445 Fifth Avenue, Suite 19F
New York, NY 10016
212-779-4977
Fax: 212-447-7277

Hyne, Eric
Encore Arts
5256 Buchanan Trail East, Suite 104
Waynesboro, PA 17268
717-765-9233
Fax: 717-765-9033

Ideno, Yoshie
707 NK Kojimachi Quarters
7-10 Sanban-cho
Chiyoda-ku Tokyo 102
Japan
81-3-3263-4813
Fax: 81-3-3263-5130

Inman, Russell
23130 Park Place Drive
Southfield, MI 48034-7110

Jacobson, William
Cyma Studios
706 Price Street
West Chester, PA 19382-2130
610-436-3492
Fax: 610-436-3352

Jacques, Wayne John, AIA
Warren Freedenfeld & Associates
39 Church Street
Boston MA 02116
617-338-0050
Fax: 617-426-2557

Jamieson, Douglas E.
827 1/2 Via de la Paz
Pacific Palisades, CA 90272
310-573-1155
Fax: 310-573-1685

Jimenez, Angelito Altares
26 Bacon Street, East Tapinac
Olongapo City, Subic Bay 2200
Philippines
6347-223-4051

Joel, J.
J. Joel & Associates
202 Brunswick Avenue
Toronto, ONT M5S 2M5
Canada
416-922-3906
Fax: 416-922-9916

Joyner, David E.
Presentation Techniques
P.O. Box 11173
Knoxville, TN 37939-1173
423-584-8334
Fax: 423-584-8334

Kariya, Takuji
1-5-5-406 Tomobuchi-cho
Miyakojima-ku Osaka 534
Japan
81-6-924-3637
Fax: 81-6-924-3287

Kim, Choong-Jin
Room #505 (Pusan Dept)
1-1, Dong Kwang-Dong Jung-Ku
Pusan 600-021
South Korea
82-51-245-7333
Fax: 82-51-245-0057

Kindred, Garfield
18557 Canal Road #3
Clinton Township, MI 48038-5821
313-263-7830
Fax: 313-263-7832

Kirchman, Robert J.
Kirchman Associates
5580 Jamestown Road
Crozet, VA 22932
804-823-2663
Fax: 804-823-6010

Kissner, Gregory R.
6544 Elmer Drive
Toledo, OH 43615
419-841-2918
Fax: 419-843-8020

Knight, Joseph C.
Knight Architects
4660 Village Court
Dunwoody, GA 30338
770-394-2798
Fax: 770-394-5311

Konishi, Hisao
741-908 Iwakami-cho
Iwakamidori Rokkaku Sagaru
Nakagyo-ku, Kyoto 604
Japan
81-75-802-2291
Fax: 81-75-802-5117

Kono, Yoshio
4.13, 3-Chome Kamirenjaku
Mitaka-shi, Tokyo 181
Japan
81-4-22-42-3795

L'Italien, Mark D.
L'Italien Architecture + Design
3740 25th Street, Suite 401
San Francisco, CA 94110
415-285-9062

La, An. S.
12 Landale Street Box, Hill 3128
Melbourne, Victoria 3128
Australia
61-3-890-7947
Fax: 61-3-890-7947

Landeck, Peter Allen
606 West 49th Terrace
Kansas City, MO 64112
816-753-8855
Fax: 816-753-8855

Landini, Tim
21211 West Ten Mile Road #507
Southfield, MI 48075

Larremore, Dean
Hampton Univ. Dept. of Architecture
Bemis Labs
Hampton, VA 23668

Law, Candace
1864 Ellwood Avenue
Berkeley, MI 48072

Lee, Sun-Ho
Suk Jun Bldg. #601
364-31 Seogko-Dong
Mapo-Ku, Seoul
Korea
82-2-334-2118x7090
Fax: 82-2-338-9416

Leong, Lawrence Ko
800 27th Avenue
San Francisco, CA 94121
415-387-6528
Fax: 415-387-6528

Lerback, Jens R.
Architectural Illustrations
5414 SW Logan Court
Portland, OR 97219
503-452-1703
Fax: 503-452-1703

Li, Wei
11 Pine Knob Drive
Albany, NY 12203
518-431-3379

Library
Canadian Centre For Architecture
1920 rue Baile
Montreal, QUE H3H 2S6
Canada
514-939-7000
Fax: 514-939-7020

Linn, Laura Clayton
Hellmuth, Obata + Kassabaum
211 North Broadway, Suite 600
St. Louis, MO 63102-2733
314-421-2010 x2476
Fax: 314-421-6073

Linton, Harold
37776 Turnberry Court
Farmington Hills, MI 48331
810-204-2864

Loli, George S.
116 St. Julien Avenue
Lafayette, LA 70506
318-232-3231

Lopez, Susan C.
Architectonic Visualizations
50 Grant Drive
Avon, CT 06001
203-673-1992

Love, Edwin
815 Ridgeleigh Road
Baltimore, MD 21212
410-377-2969

Love, Ronald J.
Ronald J. Love Architectural Illustration
3891 Bayridge Avenue
West Vancouver, BC V7V 3J3
Canada
604-922-3033
Fax: 604-922-2393

Magyar, Peter, Dr., CAHA
Spaceprint, Inc.
632 Beaumont Drive
State College, PA 16801
814-466-3054
Fax: 814-865-3289

Manus, Charles R., ASAP
Architectural Presentation Arts
43 Union Avenue #1
Memphis, TN 38103
901-525-4335
Fax: 901-527-1143

Marcincavage, George A.
16 Beekman Place
Fair Lawn, NJ 07410
201-670-9200
Fax: 201-447-3562

Margolis, John P., AIA
Margolis, Inc.
380 Boylston Street
Boston, MA 02116
617-859-2950
Fax: 617-267-6158

Maricak, Gretchen,
1040 Chapin
Birmingham, MI 48009
810-644-3001

Martyniak, Philippe
28, bd de la Croix Rousse
Lyon, 69001
France
33-72-00-87-10
Fax: 33-72-00-87-98

Matsuda, Yasuko
5-21-6, Katsutadai
Yachiyo Chiba 276
Japan
81-474-83-8574

Maurice, Scott G.
21211 West Ten Mile Road #515
Southfield, MI 48075

McBride, William A.
WAM Architectural Illustration
18 West 59th Street
Kansas City, MO 64113
816-523-2345
Fax: 816-523-2345

McBurney, James B.
1429 East River Road
Minneapolis, MN 55414
612-338-3014
Fax: 612-338-3014

McIlhargey, Robert
1639 West 2nd Avenue, Suite 410
Vancouver BC V6J 1H3
Canada
604-736-7897
Fax: 604-736-9763

McKillop, Don
One Broad Street, Suite 2
Salem, MA 01970
508-741-1362
Fax: 508-741-2081

McKinney, Santora
Hampton Univ. Dept. of Architecture
Bemis Labs
Hampton, VA 23668

Meenhorst, Loek
Loek Meenhorst Visuals
Stadhuisplein 16C Almere
Holland
31-36-5336-449
Fax: 31-36-5333-153

Melendy, Kim
21211 West Ten Mile Road #302
Southfield, MI 48075

Mergens, Beth W.
117 Johnston Court
Folsom, CA 95630
916-983-3458
Fax: 916-983-9734

Mochizuki, Ayako
13-204 Nishiisya-danchi
1-19 Kamenoi, Meito-ku
Nagoya Aichi 465
Japan
81-52-701-4235
Fax: 81-52-201-1252

Morga, Maria T.
2301 N Street NW
Washington, DC 20037
202-728-0430

Morris, Michael
21506 Syracuse Avenue
Warren, MI 48091

Morrissey, Michael B.
Michael B. Morrissey & Company
223 Indian Road Crescent
Toronto ONT M6P 2G6
Canada
416-763-1387

Mullen, Richard M.
Richard M. Mullen Presentation Art
203 West Holly Street, Suite 223
Bellingham, WA 98225
360-676-5352
Fax: 360-647-6056

Nastwold, Gail
24431 Bashian
Novi, MI 48075

Nelson, Mark, S.C., AIA
Nelson Design
3205 South Maple Avenue
Berwyn, IL 60402-2809
708-484-2720
Fax: 708-484-2730

Newton, J. Paul
Parsons Brinckerhoff
1660 Lincoln Street, Suite 2000
Denver, CO 80264
303-832-9097
Fax: 303-832-9095

Newton, Martin J.
Archimation
Kantstr. 142, Berlin 10623
Germany
49-30-312-1306
Fax: 49-30-312-1620

Nobles, David S.
Impulse Images & Animations, Inc.
9310 Autumn Sunrise
San Antonio, TX 78250
210-521-7221
Fax: 210-521-7343

Nojima, Michiko
Kosumo Kameido Bunka 205
17-12 Chome Bunka
Sumida-ku Tokyo 131
Japan
81-3-3616-1287

O'Beirne, Michael P.
42 Eighth Street #5213
Boston, MA 02129
617-846-4766

Oelfke, Don Jr.
Don Oelfke Design
P.O. Box 163746
Austin, TX 78716-3746
512-328-3381
Fax: 512-328-3381

Ogasawara, Shigeru
3-6-10-301 Kouenji Minami
Suginami-ku, Tokyo 166
Japan
81-3-3315-4569
Fax: 81-3-3315-4569

Ohm, Jerrald E.
7397 Vancouver Road
Eden Prarie, MN 55346
612-338-1634
Fax: 612-934-6964

Oles, Paul, Stevenson, FAIA
Interface Architects
One Gateway Center, Suite 501 A
Newton, MA 02158
617-527-6790
Fax: 617-527-6790

Orest Associates
3757 Main Highway
P.O. Box 809
Miami, FL 33133
305-446-8159
Fax: 305-446-8159

Ortenberg, Alexander
3190 Melanie Road
Marina, CA 93933
408-384-1174
Fax: 408-384-1174

Ostergaard, Paul B., AIA
UDA Architects
1133 Pennsylvania Avenue
Pittsburgh, PA 15222
412-765-1133
Fax: 412-765-1902

Ozawa, Kaori
3-6-10-301 Kouenji Minami
Suginami-ku, Tokyo 166
Japan
81-3-3315-4569
Fax: 81-3-3315-4569

Page, Wesley L., AIA
Hanbury Evans Newill Vlattas & Company
120 Atlantic Street, Suite 400
Norfolk, VA 23510
804-627-5775
Fax: 804-622-1012

Parker, Stephen, AIA
802 Kipling Way
St. Charles, MO 63304
314-441-8370

Payne, Hilary G.
Alto Stratus
PO Box 1266
Winchester Bay, OR 97467
503-271-7435
Fax: 503-271-7435

Peng, Gang
78 Sycamore Street #2
Somerville, MA 02145
617-666-6014
Fax: 617-666-0013

Peri, Michele
16484 Jessica
Macomb, MI 48042

Phillips, Merike
B. Phillips / M. Phillips Arch. Ill.
711 61st Street
Kenosha, WI 53143
414-658-8464
Fax: 414-658-3464

Pierson, Mark T.
21211 West Ten Mile Road #708
Southfield, MI 48075

Pillo, Amanda
Hampton Univ. Dept. of Architecture
Bemis Labs
Hampton, VA 23668

Pinto, James R.
515 West Wrightwood, Apt. 312
Chicago, IL 60614
312-929-9127

Polhemus, Rick
21211 West Ten Mile Road #515
Southfield, MI 48075

Powell, Jonathan
Hampton Univ. Dept. of Architecture
Bemis Labs
Hampton, VA 23668

Radvenis, Eugene V.
E.V. Radvenis, Inc.
1639 West 2nd Avenue, Suite 410
Vancouver BC V6J 1H3
Canada
604-736-5430
Fax: 604-736-9763

Ratner, Barbara Worth, AIA
828 Charles Allen Drive, NE
Atlanta, GA 30308
404-876-3943
Fax: 404-876-3943

Reardon, Michael
5433 Boyd Avenue
Oakland, CA 94618
510-655-7030
Fax: 510-655-7030

Regan, Eamon
Sutton Yantis Associates Architects
1952 Gallows Road, Suite 100
Vienna, VA 22182
703-734-9733
Fax: 703-847-9171

Rice, Travis
Crose-Gardner Associates, Inc.
414 61st Street
Des Moines, IA 50312
515-274-4925
Fax: 505-274-6937

Rich, Stephen W., AIA
85 Main Street
Saugus, MA 01906
617-231-0951
Fax: 617-245-6293

Ringman, Samuel C.
Ringman Design and Illustration
1800 McKinney Avenue
Dallas, TX 75201
214-871-9001
Fax: 214-871-3307

Rochon, Richard
13530 Michigan Avenue, Suite 205
Dearborn, MI 48126
313-584-9580
Fax: 313-584-4071

Rose, Ronald W. Jr.
Art Associates, Inc.
4635 West Alexis Road, PO Box 8970
Toledo, OH 43623
419-537-1303
Fax: 419-474-9113

Rost, Steve
Lawrence Tech
College of Architecture & Design
21000 West Ten Mile Road
Southfield, MI 48075

Rusch, Al, AIA
Phillips Swager Associates
3622 North Knoxville Avenue
Peoria, IL 61603
309-688-9511
Fax: 309-633-6490

Rush, Richard W.
768 North Bucknell Street
Philadelphia, PA 19130
215-763-8372
Fax: 215-763-8999

Sakal and Hood
Sakal and Hood, Architects
1012 Colley Avenue
Norfolk, VA 23507
804-622-6991
Fax: 804-622-6991

Sampson, Philip
Leo A. Daly
8600 Indian Hills Drive
Omaha, NE 68114
402-391-8111
Fax: 402-391-8564

Sanchez, John J. Jr.
11706 West 197th Street
Mokena, IL 60448
708-479-0276

Sanocki, Anne
21211 West Ten Mile Road #615
Southfield, MI 48075

Sawyer, Melissa
Hampton Univ. Dept. of Architecture
Bemis Labs
Hampton, VA 23668

Schaller, Thomas Wells, AIA
Schaller Architectural Illustration
2112 Broadway, Suite 407
New York, NY 10023
212-362-5524
Fax: 212-362-5719

Schleef, Eric C.
Eric Schleef Illustration
7740 Dean Road
Indianapolis, IN 46240
317-595-0016
Fax: 317-595-0016

Schmidt, Thomas A.
1020 Green Street #104
Honolulu, HI 96822
808-524-5524
Fax: 808-521-9016

Schneider, George A.
Watercolors By Schneider
804 South Fifth Street
Columbus, OH 43206
614-443-7014

Sedlock, Daniel
23705 Walden Court
Southfield, MI 48034

Sherrill, Thomas G.
Caperton-Johnson, Inc.
14860 Montfort, Suite 200
Dallas, TX 75240
214-991-7082
Fax: 214-991-2578

Shilletto, George
Young + Wright Architects Inc.
172 St. George Street
Toronto, ONT M5R 2M7
Canada
416-968-3522
Fax: 416-960-0172

Shimada, Kazuko
7-3-4-404 Hikarigaoka
Nerima-ku Tokyo 179
Japan
81-3-3939-8522
Fax: 81-3-3939-8522

Shirai, Hideo
Shirai Pers House
31-8-213 Honcho
Wako-shi, Saitama-ken, 351-01
Japan
81-48-465-1615
Fax: 81-48-465-1615

Shoda, Hisae
Takenaka Corporation
8-24-305, 2 Chome Deguchi
Hirakata-shi, Osaka 573
Japan
81-720-35-2690

Siriwan, Harinat F.
45 Normanby Road, North Caulfield
Melbourne, Victoria 3161
Australia
613-9576-1561
Fax: 614-1425-0892

Slutsky, Rael D., AIA
Rael D. Slutsky & Associates, Inc.
351 Milford Road
Deerfield, IL 60015
847-267-8200
Fax: 847-267-8226

Smith, Clark
63 Fulton Street
Weehawken, NJ 07087
201-902-9656
Fax: 201-974-1645

Smith, James C.
The Studio of James C. Smith
700 South Clinton Street, Suite 100
Chicago, IL 60607
312-987-0132
Fax: 312-987-0099

Smith, Peter T., AIA
Campbell / Smith Architects
PO Box 1450, 22 Depot Street
Duxbury, MA 02331
617-934-7181
Fax: 617-934-6488

Smith, Ryan
6855 Weddel
Taylor, MI 48180

Sneary, Dick
Sneary Architectural Illustration
9728 Overhill Road
Kansas City, MO 64134
816-765-7841
Fax: 816-763-0848

Sorenson, Henry
702 South 14th Street
Bozeman, MT 59715
406-587-7113

Stadler, Roger
21815 Purdue
Farmington Hills, MI 48336

Stone, Sharon M.
5050 Westgrove
Dallas, TX 75248
214-248-6520

Stracke, Charlene
1198 Larabee Lane
Howell, MI 48843-9034

Stuart, Kenneth
The Larson Company
6701 South Midvale Park Road
Tucson, AZ 85746
520-294-3900

Swaim, Matt
8090 Atlantic Blvd. C472
Jacksonville, FL 32211
904-396-3200

Swenson, Richard J.
P.O. Box 144
New Stanton, PA 15672
412-925-6387

Szasz, Peter
Peter Szasz Associates
150 Green Street
San Francisco, CA 94111
415-982-3868
Fax: 415-781-3696

Szroborz, Stanislaw W.
Atelier Szroborz
Merowingerstr. 120
Dusseldorf 40225
Germany
49-211-317-96-93
Fax: 49-211-317-95-92

Tainer, Dario, AIA
Tainer Assoiciates, Ltd.
445 West Erie Street
Chicago, IL 60610
312-951-1656
Fax: 312-951-8773

Takahata, Masakazu
1-38-21 Kuzuha Noda
Hirakata-shi
Osaka 573
Japan
81-720-57-4044
Fax: 81-720-57-8825

Tansantisuk, Mongkol, AIA
Architectural Presentations
672 Grove Street
Newton, MA 02162-1319
617-332-7885
Fax: 617-332-3789

Tappe, A. Anthony FAIA
A. Anthony Tappe Associates
6 Edgerly Place
Boston, MA 02116
617-451-0200
Fax: 617-451-3899

Tchoban, Sergei E.
NPS and Partner
Ulmenstro 40
Hamburg 22299
Germany
49-40-4806180
Fax: 49-40-470027

Thibault, Rene
407-1509 Centre Street SW
Calgary ALB T2G 2E6
Canada
403-262-4383
Fax: 403-265-4105

Thorpe, Joy
Hampton Univ. Dept. of Architecture
Bemis Labs
Hampton, VA 23668

Triplett, Kevin
79 Phillips Lane
Wrentham, MA 02093
617-423-1700
Fax: 617-451-2420

True, Todd
2 West Crestview, #17
Vernon Hills, IL 60061
708-362-6718

Tryzybowicz, Marek
Hellmuth, Obata + Kassabaum, Inc.
6688 North Central Expressway, Suite 700
Dallas, TX 75026
214-739-6688
Fax: 214-373-9523

Turner, Wendi
7604 Towering Pines Drive
Brighton, MI 48116

Uddin, Mohammed Saleh
1123 Woodhue Drive
Baton Rouge, LA 70810
504-767-3041
Fax: 504-767-3041

Ueland, Mark, AIA
Ueland, Junker & McCauley, Architects
718 Arch Street Fifth Floor
Philadelphia, PA 19106
215-440-0190
Fax: 215-440-0197

van den Hoed, Willem
1000 Huizen
Lange Geer 44, Delft, 2611 PW
The Netherlands
31-1521-33382
Fax: 31-1521-20448

Visser, Evan
3050 Gold Dust NE
Belmont, MI 49306
616-676-0890
Fax: 616-676-8159

Wakita, Masanari, JARA
1-26 Higashiyamamoto-machi Chikusa
Nagoya, Aichi 464
Japan
81-52-781-4474
Fax: 81-52-201-1252

Wakita, Osamu A.
2135 Chandeleur
Rancho Palos Verdes, CA 90275

Walker, Anthony
31433 Merriwood Park Drive
Livonia, MI 48152

Watanabe, Koji
2-20-3, Ibukino
Izumi-shi, Osaka 594
Japan
81-725-56-7608
Fax: 81-725-56-7608

Watel, Robert G. Jr.
Watel Design Communication
202 Parkland Avenue
St. Louis, MO 63122
314-821-9285
Fax: 314-821-9285

Weaver, Ralph K.
Ralph Weaver Delineator
3014 Ferguson Valley Road
McVeytown, PA 17051
717-899-6985
Fax: 717-899-5622

Wee, Andrew S.K.
453 Upper East Coast Road
#03-03 The Summit 466501
Singapore
4423115/258866
Fax: 441-6515

Wells, Jamal
Hampton Univ. Dept. of Architecture
Bemis Labs
Hampton, VA 23668

Wentworth-Sheilds, Peter
302 Main Street
Ohio, IL 61349
815-376-7111

White, Wendy Louise
Robert McIlhargey & Associates, Ltd.
1639 West 2nd Avenue, Suite 410
Vancouver BC V6J 1H3
Canada
604-731-7897
Fax: 604-736-9763

Whitman, Peter M.
Peter M. Whitman, Arch. Illustrator
77 North Washington Street
Boston, MA 02114
617-227-2932
Fax: 617-227-8316

Willis, Daniel E., AIA
1921 North Oak Lane
State College, PA 16803
814-867-5459
Fax: 814-865-3289

Windtunnel Imaging & Animation
560 Broadway, Suite 607
New York, NY 10012
212-274-1741
Fax: 212-226-2443

Wolf, Max Gandhi
2936 Morcom Avenue
Oakland, CA 94619
510-536-9850

Woodfield, Rebecca
25016 Independence Drive #9104
Farmington Hills, MI 48335

Woodhouse, Curtis James
4141 Lybyer Avenue
Miami, FL 33133
305-663-8347
Fax: 305-663-2575

Woods, Charles
Hampton Univ. Dept. of Architecture
Bemis Labs
Hampton, VA 23668

Yamada, Masaaki
Nikken Sekke
1-4-27 Koraku Bunkyo-ku
Tokyo 112
Japan
81-3-3813-3361
Fax: 81-3-3817 0755

Yamamoto, Tamotsu, ASAP
15 Sleeper Street
Boston, MA 02210
617-542-1021
Fax: 617-451-0271

Yanagida, Emiko
Hara Bldg, 4F
3-13-1 Hiroo Sibuya-ku,
Tokyo 150
Japan
81-3-3400-0371
Fax: 81-3-3498-1623

Yang, Zhengmao John
The Butner Architectural Group
300 A Water Street, Suite 200
Montgomery, AL 36104
334-264-8888
Fax: 334-834-6173

Yin, Jerry
NBBJ
111 South Jackson Street
Seattle, WA 98104
206-223-5168
Fax: 206-621-2300

Yoshida, Fujio
301, 4-7-11, Zuiko
Higashi Yodogawa-ku Osaka 533
Japan
81-6-327-4947
Fax: 81-6-327-4947

Yoshimoto, Kazunori
204 Fukuoka-chikuyu-ryo
1-2-3 Chuo, Onojo, Fukuoka 816
Japan
81-92-593-9606

Yoshimura, Tomoko
21-27 Kunimatsu-cho
Neyagawa-shi, Osaka 572
Japan
81-720-22-2557

Yu, Roger Maolin
11 Progress Avenue, Suite 200
Scarborough ONT M1P 4S7
Canada
416-609-8418
Fax: 416-609-8166

Zaleski, Serge, FSAI, ARAIA
Delineation Graphix
238 Bulwara Road
Ultimo, Sydney NSW 2007
Australia
61-2-552-3666
Fax: 61-2-692-9082

Zarzycki, Andrzej
41 Gorham Street
Somerville, MA 02144
617-776-3472

Zehnder, Matthew I.
JRA Inc.
730 West Main Street, Suite 120
Louisville, KT 40202
502-583-4697
Fax: 502-583-8576

Zimmerman, Aaron K.
120 NW Parkway
Kansas City, MO 64150
816-587-9500
Fax: 816-587-1685

Officers

Tamotsu Yamamoto	President	617-542-1021
Charles Manus	Vice-President	901-525-4335
Mongkol Tansantisuk AIA	Treasurer	617-332-7885
Robert Becker	Secretary	415-752-9946
Paul Stevenson Oles FAIA	Member-at-Large	617-527-6790

Advisory Council

Frank M. Costantino	617-846-4766
Elizabeth Ann Day	512-469-6011
Gordon Grice OAA, MRAIC	416-536-9191
William G. Hook	206-622-3849
Paul Stevenson Oles FAIA	617-527-6790
Stephen W. Rich AIA	617-231-0951
Thomas W. Schaller AIA	212-362-5524
Rael D. Slutsky AIA	847-267-8200
Dario Tainer AIA	312-951-1656

Regional Coordinators

Paul Stevenson Oles FAIA, Chairman	Boston, MA	617-527-6790
Richard Chenoweth AIA	Silver Springs, MD	301-588-0528
Stanley E. Doctor	Boulder, CO	303-449-3259
Richard B. Ferrier FAIA	Arlington, TX	817-469-8605
Robert Frank	San Francisco, CA	415-749-1418
Gordon Grice OAA, MRAIC	Toronto, ONT	416-536-9191
Sallie A. Hood	Norfolk, VA	804-622-6991
William G. Hook	Seattle, WA	206-622-3849
Harold Linton	Farmington Mills, MI	810-204-2864
Don Oelfke, Jr. AIA	Austin, TX	512-328-3381
Barbara Worth Ratner AIA	Atlanta, GA	404-876-3943
Thomas W. Schaller AIA	New York, NY	212-362-5524
Thomas Schmidt	Honolulu, HI	808-524-5524
Rael D. Slutsky AIA	Chicago, IL	847-267-8200
James C. Smith	Chicago, IL	312-987-0132
Dick Sneary	Kansas City, MO	816-765-7841
Robert G. Watel, Jr.	St. Louis, MO	314-821-9285

International Coordinators

Hans K. Chao	China	617-497-7000
Angelo DeCastro	Portugal	351-1-4671010
Robert Gill	Australia	613-826-1322
Jane Grealy	Australia	617-3394-4333
Miguelangel Gutierrez	Mexico	525-211-1921
Nobuo Kadowaki	Japan	81-3-3401-5877
Young Ki	Korea	708-843-3389
Hisao Konishi	Japan	81-75-802-2291
Sun-Ho Lee	Korea	82-27-334-2118
Philippe Martyniak	France	33-72-00-87-10
Dario Tainer AIA	Italy	312-951-1656
Sergei E. Tchoban	Germany	49-40-4806180
Willem van den Hoed	Holland	31-1521-33382

Executive Director

Alexandra Lee	Boston	617-951-1433x225